SIXTEEN
PORTRAITS

SIXTEEN PORTRAITS

of people whose houses have been preserved by The National Trust

CONTRIBUTED BY

Walter Allen
I. R. Apt
Hilton Brown
Eleanor Graham
Geoffrey Grigson
Pamela Hansford Johnson
L. P. Hartley
Professor H. Levy

Norman Nicholson
Hesketh Pearson
Stephen Potter
Sir Ronald Storrs
L. A. G. Strong
Sir Francis Tuker
Harcourt Williams
Mary Winser

EDITED BY L. A. G. STRONG

LEONARD ALFRED GEORGE

Illustrations by Joan Hassall

PUBLISHED FOR THE NATIONAL TRUST BY

The Naldrett Press

LONDON

First Published 1951
by the Naldrett Press Ltd
29 *George Street*
London, W 1

Printed in Great Britain by
RICHARD CLAY AND COMPANY LTD., BUNGAY, SUFFOLK
Printed on Mellotex Smooth White Twin Wire, made by
TULLIS RUSSELL AND CO. LTD., MARKINCH, FIFE
and set in Monotype Bembo

INTRODUCTION

THE NATIONAL TRUST is well equipped with guide books. There are several excellent volumes about the various historic houses, buildings, and stretches of country which the Trust looks after. There are a number of guide books dealing with the individual properties, and each year an up-to-date list of properties is issued. Besides all these, a new book on the general work of the Trust, written by Mr Compton Mackenzie, is being published this year.

All these publications, however, deal with places rather than with people. There is room therefore for another book concerned not so much with the houses as with the people who lived in them. Accordingly the National Trust officials gave me a list of famous names associated with houses under their care, and asked me to find a team of contributors who would each write a character sketch.

A first hope that it might be possible to write about each famous man and his house as a *gestalt*, a unit, had to be abandoned at once. Some of these famous personalities were very little affected – outwardly at any rate – by their homes. Some had only brief connections with the houses now owned by the Trust. It was clearly the best course that all the emphasis should fall on the character, that his house should take its due place in the history of his life and work, and that all temptation to give it more importance than it deserved should be resisted as a sentimental error. Even so, I would not have ventured to advise the experienced writers who have contributed to this book. I was happy to find that they reached this conclusion for themselves.

I would like to explain why, in a book which I have edited, I myself am a contributor. My agreement with the publishers required me to write one of the characters; but I should not have ventured to undertake the portrait of Thomas Hardy, had not both Lord David Cecil and Mr Cecil Day Lewis found themselves unable to write it.

I have been very glad of the chance to edit the book, because it expresses a form of piety very dear to my heart. It is good that each county, each town, each village should cherish the memory of its great sons and daughters. It is good to hear the name and place together; Browne of Tavistock, John Ford of Ilsington, Jasper Mayne of Hatherleigh. If the actual house is known, if it still stands, so much the better. These things belong to the history of our country, and they should not be forgotten.

In reminding us of such links, in pointing out the association of houses and great names, The National Trust is doing a good work. It has other objects besides the preservation of shrines. As well as wide stretches of countryside it preserves houses for their architectural and other merits; and gardens. But it is the houses we are concerned with now. These houses have to be maintained, for which purpose the writers here assembled commend The National Trust to your attention as being worthy of practical sympathy and support.

L. A. G. S.

CONTENTS

vii

ILLUSTRATIONS

By Joan Hassall

NOTE

Brief notes on The National Trust properties referred to in this book will be found at the end of each chapter. Naturally, the arrangements made with the tenants vary, so that it is not possible in this book to give a list of the times when the public may visit the properties. The reader is referred to the full list of properties, issued each year, which gives up-to-date particulars. Copies may be obtained from

The Secretary, The National Trust,
42 Queen Anne's Gate, London, S W 1
(price to non-members 2/3, post free).

24, Cheyne Row, LONDON, S W 3

THOMAS CARLYLE

By Pamela Hansford Johnson

IN spring, Thomas Carlyle sat beneath the awning in the garden, smoking his pipe and staring at the blossom – there was walnut, plum and rose, sweetbriar, jessamine, and vine – or working in hot weather at his table outdoors. From the front windows of the house there was little to see but the row of pollarded limes, and behind them a high brick wall; but Mrs Carlyle loved these limes so much that once, seeing some workmen about (as she thought) to cut them down, she rushed out on to the pavement, threatening to bring a pistol and shoot the first vandal who should lay hands on her trees.

At first sight Carlyle was much taken by Number 24,* Cheyne Row, and wrote of it with enthusiasm to his wife. He expected, as most people do and must, when moving to a new house, to be happy in it. Whether he was – or rather, to what extent, and how often he was – is a question that has passed into the fretful and distracting mysteries of literature.

He was thirty-nine years of age when he came, in June 1834, to live in Chelsea, a dour-looking man (dour is the word, and there is no sense in baulking it) with a profile like the Red Queen's for ruggedness and jut of lip. His brow was massive and bony, almost concealed by a sweep of thick, sandy hair. His eyesockets were

* It was then Number 5.

cavernous, the eye full, direct, and mournful, nose well cut and straight. Deep lines ran from the grim and deep-cleft upper lip to the protruding lower one, and the lantern-jaw gave warning of truculence and trouble. Yet there was sweetness in the face; cover up the lower part of his photograph : the nose is sensitive, the eye appealing.

'I love you, I have told you so a hundred times ... but I am not in love with you,' Jane insisted in the early and often quarrelsome days of courtship; yet in 1826, when Carlyle, exasperated, had written to tell her that if there was anyone else she wanted to marry she might as well do so and have done with it, she replied as follows : –

'Look cross at me, reproach me, even whip me, if you have the heart; your next kiss will make amends for all. But if you love me, cease, I beseech you, to make me offers of freedom; for this is an outrage which I find it not easy to forgive. If made with any idea that it is in the nature of things I should take you at your word, they do a wrong to my love, my truth, my modesty, that is, to my whole character as a woman. ... Farewell, my Be-loved. I am still yours.'

If this is not love, then we had better agree that love is unrecognizable by an outsider whatever the offered proofs, and thus open up a thousand more new literary mysteries to divert us from the essential business of studying the creative work.

The Carlyle story, though unrecognizable save as a love-story, is opaque and overcast. Carlyle was hot-blooded, impatient, irascible, dogmatic, and, in social converse, highly intolerant of opinions other than his own. The same may be said for Jane. They were too similar; and inevitably they clashed. Froude, whose biography of Carlyle called forth such a storm of protest, may have been ruthless, insensitive, and, worse, the possessor of an unreliable memory; but *My Relations with Carlyle* has the stamp of an honest man angrily justifying what he believes to be the truth, and makes the whole attack upon him bear a certain resemblance to the attacks by enraged Dickensians upon Miss Gladys Storey's *Dickens and Daughter* – a work which, by the honesty of its revelations, opened up an entirely new field of Dickensian criticism.

Now Jane Welsh Carlyle, though not a beautiful woman, had very considerable physical attraction. She was witty, shrewd, and brilliant, and if her tongue was not infrequently a cruel one, this is no new thing among wits. To any person of high conversational and epistolary brilliance, the temptation to be spiteful upon occasion is not merely strong: it is irresistible. A joke is often far too good to spoil or to repress, and saints are few. Women of Jane's type often exhibit neurotic symptoms of a kind similar to hers. Jane suffered appallingly from migraine, and may have suffered also from a mild manic depressive cycle. Indeed, it is possible to argue that brilliance, unless it springs out of darkness, gives the impression of being no more than giddiness and lightness of mind; really contagious high spirits usually arise from a schism in the personality.

Thomas, however, though moody, does not appear to have been erratic in Jane's sense; even his quarrelsomeness was always predictable. He worked with a kind of violent concentration, and it is noteworthy that the time he most bitterly hurt Jane was when he replied, to her confession that she had once made up her mind to leave him and marry someone else, 'Well, I do not know that I should have missed you; I was very busy then with my *Cromwell.*'

But women who marry great men should know what to expect. The 'artistic temperament' is much more than, as has been suggested, a synonym for Temper: and the temperament of genius is so rooted in self-absorption that it makes exorbitant demands, both consciously and unconsciously, upon devotion and love. That Carlyle did, on one occasion at least, physically ill-use Jane, leaving bruises on her arms, seems not to be in dispute; but then, Jane could be provocative and infuriating, and a man goaded into shaking her may quite well have used more violence than he intended. One may not excuse it; but it is unjustifiable to write a man down, because of a moment's fury, as a monster of brutality.

Carlyle was nothing of the kind. His letters to his wife are full of a deep love and respect – not only of that respect which must exist between men and women who have passed through innumerable emotional crises together, but profound intellectual respect also. And it is this respect that leads us to the curious business of Lady Harriet Baring, afterwards Lady Ashburton.

Now Froude, and subsequent writers, have suggested that Carlyle was a husband only in name, and that this failure lay at the root of the troubles between him and Jane. Froude, indeed, reports that 'the morning after his wedding-day he tore to pieces the flower-garden at Comeley Bank in a fit of ungovernable fury.'

Kay Dick, in a sensible and excellent preface to *A Selection from the Letters and Memorials of Jane Welsh Carlyle*, makes this interesting point. 'What has never been suggested – and what is a most astounding omission – is that the lack of children in the Carlyle ménage lay not with Carlyle but with Jane. With her curious and baffling medical history, is it not feasible to suppose that Jane may have been sterile?'

This question of their childlessness, however, is something apart from the question of their physical happiness. The truth is unguessable, and we must let it lie; whatever the secret, there must have been some disastrous maladjustment of this nature behind the life at Cheyne Row.

Now a woman of Jane's type, feeling herself unsatisfied or unable to satisfy, takes refuge and comfort in her intellectual force and charm. She was one of the finest letter-writers who ever lived, a delightful hostess and an enthralling conversationalist. Her wit darted, sparkled, and glanced from any given stimulus, like sunlight flashing off water. It was essential to her that she should, in all these respects, be unrivalled and incomparable in her husband's eyes. As Miss Dick writes: –

'Jane's particular aptitude was that throughout her life Great Men would come to her to be applauded, only too soon themselves to render homage. At this point Jane's special weakness must be exhibited, if only because this very weakness contained her charm: Jane was a flirt, but a particular kind of flirt. ... The power to charm and bind was Jane's most feminine quality, and allied as it was, in later years, to an intellectual power, it

B

would be extraordinary had Jane not tested her ability in this direction now and again.'

Jane, then, had to appear as the central female figure in any group. She had to show her husband the authority of her charm, and hold him by it. If she failed, the magic would go from their lives, and there would be nothing left between them but the sourness, the quarrels, and the bitterness.

Carlyle came of peasant stock, and because of his genius, rose out of it to astonishing heights of fame. The famous came to Number 24, Cheyne Row to pay court to him – Tennyson, Browning, Dickens, Huxley, Ruskin, Leigh Hunt: and Chopin played on Mrs Carlyle's piano. The fact that early circumstances had given him a taste for modest living – in his richest days he would never employ more than one servant, and the housekeeping arrangements were frugal – he could not help but enjoy his own eminence, taking pride in the admiration of 'great' men and women, and of men and women in London 'Society'. Such admiration is the seal of success. It is the soul's assurance. It would be unnatural for anyone of such small beginnings not to derive some satisfaction from it.

So it was that Carlyle became profoundly flattered and delighted by the friendship of the clever, witty, original, and accomplished Lady Harriet Baring. He never, of course, became her lover; but it is extremely probable that the strong intellectual and emotional sympathy between them did awaken in Carlyle some impulse of romantic love. For the first time Jane had found herself with a rival in her own field, and one who could rob her of the one thing she most deeply prized: the status in her husband's eyes of the *only woman* with the brains and the heart to understand. She had taken consolation from her queenship. It was a psychological necessity that she should reign. Now Carlyle was making her divide her throne.

Sir James Crichton-Browne, supporting his attack on Froude's interpretation of this affair, quotes letters from Jane to Carlyle, in which she expresses friendly sentiments towards Lady Harriet. Certainly she was often her guest. Is it to be expected, however, that a woman of Jane's courage and generosity would not have tried, at least, to come to terms with her own jealousy, and have tried to share fully in the friendship, turning it safely into a three-cornered one? For Jane not to have been bitterly hurt and made bitterly jealous by her husband's absorbed affection for Lady Harriet and his confidence in her, would have been impossible, taking into account Jane's temperament and the physical difficulties of the marriage. Lady Harriet must have seemed to her to have all the advantages: worldly position, good health (Jane's was wretched), and social confidence. Only a thoroughly insensitive person would not have been jealous in the circumstances, and Jane was sensitive and in love.

That Number 24, Cheyne Row was the scene of great suffering we cannot doubt: but it was also the scene of love, that peculiar and indestructible love, the compound of *l'amour passion* and *l'amour-goût*, which outlasts physical and vanity-love, and renders even old age radiant by its afterglow.

In ordinary social life Carlyle was an easy-going man,

loving company, but asking the company to accept his ways, rather than putting himself out to please it. He would stretch himself on the drawing-room floor with a cushion between the wall and his back, resting the bowl of his long clay pipe in the fireplace so that the fumes might not disturb his wife, while she would lie on the sofa near him. When he was not thundering or dogmatizing – which he usually was – he would tell excellent stories; and Jane would talk with glitter and freedom, sharpening her wit upon his as he upon hers. In the earlier years, porridge was always served at eleven o'clock every evening; and Leigh Hunt, at any rate, enjoyed it.

Both Carlyles suffered from insomnia, and the record of the sleepless nights of these two neurotic people is sad reading. Dogs barked out at the back; at dawn the cocks crew, and the hens in the nearby coops awoke refreshed and vocal. It is doubtful whether either Thomas or Jane would have slept more soundly in padded rooms; but the insomnia-victim is always attaching to external causes the misery which is hatched deep and solitary in his own brain.

Carlyle was dyspeptic. His temper was, upon occasion, appalling; but in essentials he was a kind man who could be – though not always – abnormally sensitive to the feelings of others. (It is a mistake to regard sensitivity as a constant virtue.) The famous story of his almost incredible kindness to John Stuart Mill, when Mill came to report that the manuscript of *The French Revolution*, while in his charge, had been burned to ashes by the housemaid, demonstrates the heights of forbearance to which a passionate man may climb; even if we hold the view that there are some disasters which one takes well because they are too atrocious to take ill, Carlyle's behaviour remains impressive.

He worked at terrific emotional tension. The creative impetus was an agony; and also an absorbing pleasure. It is impossible to read *The French Revolution* without understanding something of the mental process that forced it on to the page. Good history it is not, for Carlyle took the simple view that the Revolution was simply a divine punishment for the vice and laxity of the eighteenth century, and the serious historian looks for causes of a more precise nature. (Also, the most important and productive research into the period, especially with reference to Danton and the fall of the Gironde, was made long after Carlyle's death.) *The French Revolution* is, however, a most extraordinary translation of the writer's vision. Violent, exhortatory, demagogic, superbly pictorial, it has something in common with the first-class film script: all the time we are made to *see*, until our very eyes seem to tire and we close the book, exhausted not so much by the print, but by the succession of tremendous pictures that have been flashed ceaselessly across our imagination. Such writing springs from absolute intensity of thought, thought that never remains on one level, but all the time drills deeper and painfully deeper, to wring from the mind the last image and the last cry.

A writer who drives his mind at such tension is unlikely to have much driving-force left over for discovering the whims, needs, discontents, and sorrows of the human beings near to him. At least, he is unlikely to expend it during the period of creative activity.

Genius should not, perhaps, marry genius: and Jane, too, had genius in her own way. She was capable of as deep a sensitivity as Carlyle, but hers was operating – undistracted by artistic creation – *all* the time. Yet he might have found a lesser woman, a mere ministrant to his comfort and solace to his barren hours, intolerable. The tie between Thomas and Jane was irrefragible. Whatever happened on the surface or below it, the rope stayed taut.

The trouble is that being a wit and a housewife are not all-absorbing occupations; being a creative writer must be, for a large part of the time. A feeling that she was neglected made Jane irascible and anxious, and she wrote in this mood to her husband just at the time when he was completing *Cromwell* :–

'My Dear – I find you excessively provoking. Now that you are done with your work, why cannot you *appoint* a day for coming off? I made sure of knowing by to-day's Letter when you would come: and not a word on the subject!

'I have been to Liverpool. Started before the post came in, and was flying back faster than the horses to get your Letter; and *voilà!* Speculations about dining with Scott, Browning, etc., etc. I am quite angry and that is the truth of it; for if I had thought you were to dawdle so long I would have been at home with you by this time. The worst for *you* is, that I have not time to subside; for the starting hour of the post is just at hand. Certainly I did not expect you *this* week; but I expected to have got by this time a "fixed point" for my expectation.

'I would not have written at all till I could write in better humour and with greater deliberation, but you said something about "morbid fancies", and I am not disappointed enough to wish to inflict such on you while there is a minute's time left to hinder them.

'Yours, in a breakneck haste,

'J.C.'

This may be the kind of letter a woman writes to a neglectful man; but it is also the kind she writes only to a man who has rendered her deeply and forever in love with him, and who has captured the full tide of her imagination.

To this reproachful note Carlyle replied with humour and tenderness; but before she received the reply, she had written him an apology for her little burst of ill-temper.

With regard to Carlyle's approach to friendly and social relations, Froude makes one interesting point. How often have we heard one person say of another, 'He's all right *when you're alone with him*'? In the company of several people, Carlyle could never still the demagogic side of his tongue, turning such social occasions into public meetings. He denounced (in monologue) 'all manner of things and persons'; he was overbearing, arrogant, and as convinced as Charles I of his own inevitable rightness in whatever he did. For such temperaments as his the impulse to 'hold court' is irresistible. There are only two desirable sounds: one's own voice, and all the other voices in respectful unison. Carlyle loved to be the soloist, turning his friends into a not very hard-working chorus. Yet alone with a single companion, Froude tells us, 'he was delightful, brilliantly entertaining, sympathetic, and even occasionally tolerant of what at other times he would execrate, and full of the widest information about all things and subjects'.

The cockatoo impulse often belongs with the temperament of great men who, perhaps, realizing their greatness, see no reason why they should not get some fun out of it.

And Carlyle had little enough fun. Shut in his soundproof room, he would remain dead to the world; while his wife, often bored and neuralgic, entertained the visitors 'of whom she dared not ask him to relieve her'. Though there seems no reason to doubt Froude on this subject, he certainly does use it as a stick with which to beat Carlyle. The point is that, for the artist, work properly comes first; and there was no reason at all why Carlyle should have emerged from it for the benefit of callers. It is highly likely that Jane, with her intelligence and imaginative sympathy, did not fail to appreciate this point.

She loved and admired him; if she occasionally confessed herself bored with the oft-repeating (for the visitors' benefit) of the same story, or wished he would moderate his violent flow of oratory, it was only natural. There are wives of many public men who must have felt precisely the same. But wishing a person were otherwise is a very different thing from expecting him to become so, or attempting to remodel him.

Carlyle had to the last, according to Froude, 'the manners of an Annandale peasant'. He never learned, as

Jane did, the social graces. He was uncouth and inconsiderate; he was also tender and full of natural goodness, attentive – often painfully so – to the demands of a very active conscience. When Jane died he grieved for her bitterly. Everything he had ever done to hurt her, however petty, however unintentional, haunted his mind. He longed to call back the past, to be with her again, to offer her all the outward kindnesses and marks of love which she had craved – to be, in short, an ordinary husband. A man without genius. A man who could never have written *Frederick* or *The French Revolution*.

Certainly, in his later years, he became more tolerant and more lovable. Froude came to offer him love; hitherto he had been able to offer only admiration. Froude wrote of him with a frankness that aroused the most devastating censure; but in what he wrote love and devotion are apparent always. Certainly he darkened the total picture. There was sorrow at Number 24, Cheyne Row. There was anger and bitterness. But there was also fun, sociability, affection, and a kind of ineradicable youthful tomfoolery; some of the letters that passed between Thomas and Jane in middle age might have been written by a boy and girl insecurely and richly in love. Above all there was that tie which sometimes comes to exist between two people, making them, despite fret and frustration and pain, not one flesh, but one spirit; a single spire of flame.

Carlyle's House, London, S W 3

Cheyne Row is a street running north and south from King's Road to Cheyne Walk. No. 24 is on the east side and about the middle house of the street; it is one of a block of a dozen red-brick houses dating from 1708. It is open as a Carlyle Museum.

S. T. COLERIDGE

By Stephen Potter

At the end of the year 1796 there was developing, in the home of the S. T. Coleridges, a situation of the kind which has come to be known as Coleridgean.

Coleridge had been married for more than two years, and this marriage, as he had told his friends, was delightfully happy. Its beginning was inauspicious. The long engagement started amidst all the ardours of Coleridge's first friendship with Southey, when the two young men pledged each other that they would find themselves mates to take with them to the new self-governing colony they were going to found on the banks of the Susquehannah. But in spite of the fact that the collapse of the scheme had caused Coleridge to look with a more detached and critical eye on the rather low intellectual and social qualifications of Miss Fricker and her ambition for a refined and respectable home, Coleridge, once he had been pushed, nagged, and cold-shouldered as it were to the altar, decided that he was happy. There was a cottage smothered in roses, the scene was rural but Bristol and the Redcliffe Library were not too far distant, friends turned up to distract him pleasantly from work, and Coleridge went off with them on long tours, and returned from one of these to find himself the father of a son.

Yet in December 1796, though the marriage was still

Coleridge's Cottage, NETHER STOWEY, SOMERSET

happy, it did not seem perfect. Sarah was pretty, and loving, but she was impatient as well. She was married to a genius, of course, but genius must be helped by what Coleridge was beginning to call 'that vulgar article of life – bread'. Coleridge's paper *The Watchman*, which he had tried to edit, write, and sell more or less single-handed, had failed. Cottage, wife, and child may have been all that they should be, Coleridge had endless time to work, but in spite of plans and promises no writing came.

Coleridge did what he was so often to do again in similar circumstances. He created a difficulty. He decided to move house. He had met a new friend – Thomas Poole of Nether Stowey, by the Quantock Hills. Thomas Poole, he knew, owned a tiny house adjoining the back of his garden. It was vacant. The Coleridges must be his tenants. Coleridge wrote to say so.

Poole was not so certain the idea was a good one. Coleridge as a visitor – yes. But Coleridge and the Coleridge family outside his back door – he was not so sure. Was it wise of Coleridge to separate himself from his friends, and from his library? And was not this roadside cottage too small even for Coleridge's wants? How would Coleridge be able to write, said Poole, between roadway and wife, baby and the back kitchen?

But Coleridge, at once, and therefore, became utterly determined. He would be author no longer but would make money by cultivating vegetables in the garden. Poole was still doubtful and Coleridge wrote again: –

'I wrote the former letter immediately on receipt of yours, in the first flutter of agitation. The tumult of my spirits has now subsided, but the Damp struck into my very heart; and there I feel it. O my God! my God! where am I to find rest? Disappointment follows disappointment, and Hope seems given me merely to prevent my becoming callous to Misery. Now I know not where to turn myself. I was on my way to the City Library, and wrote an answer to it there. Since I have returned I have been poring into a book, as a shew for not looking at my wife and the baby. By God! I dare not look at them. Acton! The very name makes me grind my teeth! What am I to do there? ...

'Pardon, if I write vehemently. I meant to have written calmly; but bitterness of soul came upon me. Mrs. Coleridge has observed the workings of my face while I have been writing, and is entreating to know what is the matter. I dread to show her your letter. I dread it. My God! my God! What if she should dare to think that my most beloved friend has grown cold towards me! ...'

I quote this letter at length because its tone, and the situation which produced it, are typical of so much in Coleridge's character. The excess of feeling, the self-dramatization, the inappropriate agonies, and above all the creation of difficulty perfectly illustrate one side of his nature.

Coleridge is certainly not the only writer to suffer from this disease of authorship. Faced with blank sheets of paper, a fine theme, freely chosen by himself, and an infinity of time for work, Coleridge was often incapable of one word. But give him the back of an envelope, already scrawled upon, or the narrowest margins of a printed book held with difficulty on his knees while the coach jolted over the roughest roads, and the sentences began to flow.

Coleridge was always accusing himself of idleness. 'Oh wayward and desultory spirit of genius, ill canst thou brook a taskmaster,' he would say. Or 'There is a vice of such powerful venom that one grain of it will poison the overflowing goblet of a thousand virtues'. Sometimes he would be more realistic about it. There should be a hospital for lunacy and idiocy of the *will*, he wrote. Had such a house of health been in existence 'I know who would have entered himself as a patient'.

Yet words like indolence and ineffectiveness cannot truly be applied to the results of work so nobly voluminous, nor to a man who overcame such real psychological difficulties so triumphantly.

What is true is that Coleridge needed the spur of these difficulties. Coleridge himself told Hazlitt that he 'liked to compose in walking over uneven ground, or breaking through the straggling branches of a copse-wood'. He would set himself large tasks, 'spawning plans like a her-ring', as Southey said, in the hope that he would be thereby spurred to the achievement of one of them. His best lectures were unprepared, or long digressions from the announced subject. The only regular Coleridge pub-lication which achieved any length of life, the *Friend*, was written, printed, and sold at places many miles apart, and separated by high Westmorland mountains which the editor and author had to clamber across on his own rheumatic feet.

This trait in Coleridge was the explanation of this habit of making a tragic crisis out of such a problem as moving house. It was the predominating eccentricity which explains so many of the Coleridgean characteristics so distasteful to his friends.

For Coleridge, continually aware of these flaws in his character, was continuously veering between the two opposite extremes, equally embarrassing to his audience, of self-depreciation and self-justification. He would write long letters of self-abasement, acknowledging that he had 'played the fool with his inheritance', and then next day he would be all excessive nobility and high mindedness. 'It is some consolation – nay, a great consolation', he writes to Charles Lamb, 'to know that my difficulties have not fallen on me thro' any vice, any extravagance or self-indulgence, but only from having imprudently hoped too highly of men ...' Sometimes the magnificent and eloquent voice seems to thin to the cadences of Micawber, if not of Pecksniff. 'What are our lives? Accidents,' he would say. Or 'My dear Sir, am I under the inebriation of Self-conceit? I trust not.'

All this tested the loyalty of Coleridge's friends, and helps to account for the later coldness of Southey and the more violent and irritable defection of former admirers like Hazlitt.

The loyalty of his own children must have been severely tested too, for he was never more unbendingly noble in tone than when he was addressing Derwent or poor Hartley. His manner was perhaps particularly unattractive to women, and there were many of them who failed to be drawn under the Coleridge spell. To these, Coleridge was that worst of failures, the pseudo-genius. As Kitty Wedgwood wrote: –

'I cannot overcome the first disagreeable impression of his accent and exterior. I confess too ... there is in my opinion too great a parade of superior feeling; and an excessive goodness and sensibility is put forward, which gives an appearance, at least, of conceit, and excites suspicion that it is acting; as real sensibility never endeavours to excite notice ...'

That is a fair summary of Coleridge's character as it appeared to many of his contemporaries, and to some more recent judges. But what a fate awaits the critic who presents this side of him as if it was Coleridge as he was – as if it was the 'real' Coleridge. What a judgement such a critic will call forth on himself.

For the truth is that the real Coleridge, to which these flaws were irrelevantly and absurdly attached throughout his life, was something far different – the true genius to which this false imitation of the mannerisms of genius was attached. Indeed it is possible to write another 'character of Coleridge' in which the various traits, even the faults themselves, seem transmuted and transformed into examples of human nature at its highest.

Coleridge as a young man, we know, seemed the personification of youthful genius. When his light shone, he seemed inspired. It was said that he wrote always 'from the depths of his being', but this deep-rootedness of thought, this power to go beyond the pros and cons of ordinary argument to a principle which lay deeper than either, was even more apparent in his talk.

The young men saw in Coleridge one who had achieved young manhood in all its power and richness – a Coleridge ardent and believing, eloquent and sensitive, and changing and adapting with the fluidity of life. 'His genius at that time had angelic wings, and fed on manna.' He talked for ever, said Hazlitt, and you wished him to talk for ever. His thoughts did not come with labour 'but as if borne on the gusts of genius'. 'Poetry and Philosophy had met together. Truth and Genius had embraced, under the eye and with the sanction of Religion.'

Sometimes, very often in his middle life, the light in Coleridge seemed to be turned out. Then, it is true, the discourse continued but only the padded framework remained. The old subjects, Reason and Understanding, Fancy and the Imagination, continued to revolve, but as repetitions only. Naturally the young men as they grew older concluded that the Coleridgean fountain had dried up for ever and went away complaining, like Southey, of the 'endless loquacity'. A tradition grew up which has never quite died – that Coleridge's genius came to an end with the last of the famous poems, that after 1804 Coleridge was critical and 'philosophical' merely; his inspiration had gone.

But in fact not only did Coleridge's genius never die, as Wordsworth's died; it retained its power and its youthfulness till his death. Charles Lamb almost alone of his contemporaries realized the extraordinary power that remained in Coleridge. 'I cannot think a thought, I cannot make a criticism on men and books,' he wrote at the time of Coleridge's death, 'without an effectual turning and reference to him.' And at Highgate, at the end of his life, the young men were flocking to hear the great voice just as they had come to Nether Stowey a generation before, to hear him, as Carlyle heard him, 'like a sage escaped from the inanity of life's battle, and attracting towards him the thoughts of innumerable brave souls still engaged there'.

This power of youth in Coleridge showed itself most strongly, most beyond even the powers common to genius, in his continued ability to *change*. Coleridge's topographical wanderings in space were often unhappy and not very fruitful, and frequently concerned with a fruitless desire to escape from his own bad habits or his own unhappy family. His spiritual journey, on the other hand, is an epitome of man's unique power to widen the boundaries of his world.

Coleridge begins his articulate life as the youthful cynic and Voltairean sceptic. Then comes the period of political idealism associated, like so many of his meta-morphoses, with a new friend, Southey. Political and social equality is the ideal, the new republic of Pantiso-cracy must be founded. Coleridge is at his most scorn-fully powerful at this period.

'It is wrong, Southey! for a little girl with a half-famished sickly baby in her arms to put her head in at the window of an inn – "Pray give me a bit of bread and meat!" from a party dining on lamb, green peas, and salad. Why? Because it is impertinent and obtrusive!'

A 'very intelligent young man', says Coleridge, re-commends the Susquehannah as a site for the new pro-ject because of its excessive beauty, its security from hos-tile Indians and the attacks of bison, and because 'literary characters make money there'.

But never, says Coleridge, 'can I remember those

35

days with either shame or regret. For I was most sincere, most disinterested! My opinions were indeed in many and most important points erroneous; but my heart was single.'

Coleridge attacked the next great change in his life with equal vigour. He becomes a philosopher after the School of Hartley. 'I am a complete necessitarian,' he says. A few months later philosophic doubts creep in, all to be swept away in a new great friendship, with Wordsworth, and a new influence, through Wordsworth, of the external world, of Nature. For Coleridge now, the 'huge amphitheatre of rich and elmy fields' seems like society –

> Conversing with the mind, and giving it
> A livelier impulse and a dance of thought!

So far the processes of Coleridge's growth can be paralleled by many English poets. In the next stage, which he almost but perhaps never quite completed, Coleridge stepped beyond all but a very few. He turned to philosophy once more, but this time not to find a new theory but to find himself.

Coleridge has never been more persistently misunderstood than by those who have tried to follow this last phase of his evolution. Coleridge, true to his character, created unnecessary difficulties for himself by hiding the extraordinary lucidity of his thought in a style without a framework, long sentences undermined by endless parentheses, and a vocabulary of his own invention in which uncommon and complicated meaning was given to some of the simplest words in the language. But once the thread of Coleridge's thought is disentangled, the words reveal Coleridge as the greatest of the English mystics.

Coleridge was approaching the age of thirty when disaster came to interrupt this spiritual evolution. In the middle period of his life, the Coleridgean flaws and weaknesses gained the upper hand. But even in these years of disappointment and failure, Coleridge never lost his powers of self-knowledge. His friends and critics accounted for Coleridge's eclipse in their own ways. An unhappy marriage, illness, his thwarted love for Sara Hutchinson, his jealousy of Wordsworth, his quarrel with him, the ravages of opium.[1]

But Coleridge's own story is the only one that counts. Not only in the *Ode to Dejection*, but in notes and letters, he has left us the most moving of all accounts of the descent to the Valley of the Shadow. It is the fact that this courage of self-knowing never left him which made possible Coleridge's brave recovery.

*   *   *

Thomas Poole relented in the end, and Coleridge came to live at Nether Stowey. Coleridge's instinct was right,

---

[1] Too much has been made of the effect of drugs on Coleridge at this time. But it is interesting to note how closely the medical description of morphia poisoning parallels Coleridge's self-analysis in the *Ode to Dejection*.   Here is the clinical picture:—

'Will power is completely paralysed. ... The perpetual fight between the necessity for decision and the incapacity for it, as well as the consciousness of inferiority and misery with which the victim is obsessed, cause terrible suffering. Even in his dreams this mental torture is continued, for the happy, delightful past is brought into tormenting comparison with the despair of the present. ...

'In the case of such persons every contact with the higher sentiments, love of the family, good humour, faith, reverence, the beauty of nature and the activities of human life is lost ...'

(From Dr Lewin: *Phantastica*.)

for the months at Stowey were far the happiest and most productive of his life. Here flourished at its best the greatest friendship of his life, with the Wordsworths. Here he was given by a few perceptive followers the kind of recognition he always longed for. Here he wrote the *Ancient Mariner*.

The *Ancient Mariner* is one of the most popular and most read poems ever written – by one of our least read and most neglected authors. Those who wish to get the best from Coleridge must go beyond the *Ancient Mariner* to those long letters, filled to the crowded margins of the paper, or to the Notebooks, where Coleridge pours out – himself. Coleridge, in everything he wrote, wore his heart on his sleeve, and this is the most valuable quality in his character. He shows us the depths of human weakness and the heights of human strength. Thereby he reflects and describes for us the failures and the potentialities of our own nature.

Coleridge's Cottage, Somerset

At the west end of Nether Stowey village, which lies eight miles west of Bridgwater. A small, unpretentious cottage where the poet lived from 1796 to 1800. It houses a small collection of Coleridge relics.

Flatford Mill, SUFFOLK

JOHN CONSTABLE

By Geoffrey Grigson

THERE is a celebrated story of a meeting between Blake the spiritual artist and John Constable the terrestrial artist of cloud and the cloud-sprinkled landscape. Blake picked out a drawing by Constable of fir-trees on Hampstead Heath and declared it was not drawing, it was inspiration. Constable replied with his rather sharp, dry common-sense that he never knew it before; it was meant for drawing.

There you have Constable, the careful son of the well-to-do country miller of East Bergholt (where he was born in 1776, though not in the mill house at Flatford which he painted nor in Willy Lott's house which appears in 'The Hay Wain', which are both among the houses of the National Trust). He had much in him of the directness and also of the complexity of the country-man, especially when his own deep interests were in doubt. He was both proud and humble, sarcastic and affirmative, enigmatic and simple. The pride, the sarcasm, the enigmatic aloofness were the ramparts of defence, the walls, strongly manned, around the gravity of his vision; and the mixture makes Constable far more attractive than the engaging simpleton he has been transformed into by legend. Ruskin, who disliked Constable's work, held that a painter has no other business than to see and feel. He held that Constable perceived in a landscape about as much as might be apprehended by an intelligent fawn and a skylark. He may not have been altogether wrong. But perhaps, as we all have been, Ruskin was affected too much by the life of Constable which his friend C. R. Leslie compiled with the most pious and evasive skill.

Long ago the Redgrave brothers complained that Leslie had painted Constable *couleur de rose*. 'The landscape painter,' they wrote, 'though of a manly nature, was eminently sarcastic, and was very clever at saying the bitterest things in a witty manner.' And they added that this had no doubt been increased 'by the neglect with which the would-be connoisseurs had treated his art, and by the sneers of commonplace critics'. Half a century or so later Constable's unexpurgated letters to Leslie were published, and the legend of the simpleton from East Bergholt was destroyed finally. Constable was a fighter in defence of deep intuitions.

Painting in the open, staring at clouds, at the sparkle of vegetation and water, he was possessed. Standing in his London painting-room, preparing a new large canvas for the Academy or the British Institution, he kept half an eye upon climbing into repute, and so compromised a little with his vision. He lacked the bluntness, the intolerance, and the boldness of Courbet blundering and bellowing like a bull among the sham idealisms of French painting in the fifties and sixties. We have to reckon that he was the son of a cautious business-man and was well aware of the value of money and esteem. He was pricked privately and publicly as a man who inhabited the lower walks of society and of art. When he engaged himself to

Maria Bicknell, granddaughter of the wealthy rector of Bergholt, he was not only the miller's son, he was not only a painter (a profession none too highly regarded. Painters had joined in the Academy to raise their social status and to be able to write 'Esq.' after their names as well as 'R.A.'), but a painter who was unsuccessful.

In the art society of London he was something of an obstinate original, respected a little, criticized still more, and unable at the first and the second attempt to find a single Academician who would vote to make him an Associate. The one thing he desired in life and in painting was (in a phrase of Pope's which he employed) 'the calm sunshine of the heart'. To gain it, he had to gain a wife against opposition. To gain a wife and give her support and to quieten the doubts of the miller's son turned painter, he yearned after professional success.

No one could say of him as Scott wrote of Turner, that his 'palm was as itchy as his fingers were ingenious'; but he was torn between his difficulties and his intuition. Turner was tougher, harder, and less volatile. In the earlier years when Turner and his landscape followers were being called 'The White Painters' for their rejection of the old school of landscape whose pictures moved from conventional dark to conventional light, and when Turner was criticized for 'blotching', for a vicious lack of equal 'finishing', for undesirable novelty, and for brightness of colour, Constable still sided somewhat with reaction; but as he found himself, his own parallel novelty and freshness were assailed and his tongue sharpened in reply. He had to maintain his truth and, with his will and against it, struggle at the same time after that professional

43

status represented in those days by the letters A.R.A. and then R.A.

They made him A.R.A. in 1819; for full membership they kept him waiting another ten years. Constable reveals himself during that period – in which success and failure, exultation and depression, security and disaster, happiness and black unhappiness all attend him. A number of his notes to Leslie have to do with this distasteful business of proceeding to R.A. The Academicians had to be canvassed. Several he called upon either talked of high art or kept the door closed to him. 'I have heard so much of the higher walks of the art, that I am quite sick. I had my own opinions even on that – but I was desired to hold my tongue and not *argue the point*.' Landscape was the lower walk; and for the connoisseurs' taste Constable painted too much greenery, too many barges, locks, stumps, and water-weeds. A connoisseur's poem urged that painters must pursue idealisms and fauns and fairies, Ariosto and Greek fables, sacred histories and sublimities of blood and darkness. Then the poem rounded upon Constable, who had lately exhibited 'The Lock' and 'The Leaping Horse': –

> Learn this, ye painters of dead stumps,
> Old barges and canals, and pumps,
> Paint something fit to see, no view
> Near Brentford, Islington, or Kew –
> Paint anything, – but what you do.

Still, if Constable was to be an R.A. he had to swallow something of his own disdain and endure the taste. 'I called on Bone. He wanted not to see me. I called on Cooke. He would not see me – but that may not be conclusive; though perhaps in the great Bone there may be a fracture.' It was no good. 'Highminded members who stickel for the "elevated and noble" walks of art – i.e. preferring the *shaggy posteriors* of a *Satyr* to the moral feelings of *Landscape'* – had preferred also to elect William Etty.

If there were two kinds of picture Constable distrusted they were the agitated and over-populated effort at wild sublimity and the glossy, feminized allegory; and Etty painted both kinds. Of the sublime (though he was probably thinking of John Martin and his Old Testament immensities, and not of Etty), Constable once quoted from the 1st Book of Kings, 'A great and strong wind rent the mountains, and brake in pieces the rocks before the Lord; but the Lord was not in the wind; and after the wind an earthquake; but the Lord was not in the earthquake: and after the earthquake a fire; but the Lord was not in the fire; and after the fire *a still small voice*.' The collector and connoisseur Robert Vernon bought Etty's 'Youth on the Prow and Pleasure at the Helm', glossy with naked nymphs, which is now in the National Gallery. Later he acquired Constable's 'Valley Farm'. Etty's picture he moved to a better place, giving the old position to the landscape. Constable commented broadly and caustically upon this removal in one of his notes to Leslie, talking of 'Etty's "Bumboat"'; on another occasion, thinking of his nudes, he wrote blandly of Etty as a procurer.

Within all these bristling defences lie Constable's own statements about his work, and the work itself, which is finally the crystallization of his character. Within all the idealistic shams of his day he knew, in a phrase which is usually misquoted, that there was 'room for a natural painture', an honest art obedient to the nature before one's eyes, or, as he qualified it, 'a pure and unaffected representation of the scenes that may employ me'. He possessed indeed the purest eye with which he never saw, as he remarked, an ugly thing in his life, because nothing was ugly. 'How much I can imagine myself with you,' he wrote to his friend Fisher in 1821, 'on your fishing excursion in the New Forest. What river can it be? But the sound of water escaping from mill-dams, etc., etc., Willows, old rotten Planks, slimy posts and brickwork, I love such things. ... Still I should paint my own places best; painting is with me but another word for feeling, and I associated "my careless boyhood" with all that lies on the banks of the Stour; those scenes made a painter, and I am grateful.' He put down a note for himself that 'The world is wide; no two days are alike, nor even two hours; neither was there ever two leaves of a tree alike since the creation of the world; and the genuine productions of art, like those of nature, are all distinct from each other.' And he told Leslie that his 'limited and abstracted art is to be found under every hedge and in every lane, and therefore nobody thinks it worth picking up'. In another letter: 'It is time at 56 to begin at least to *know oneself* – and' – putting it modestly – 'I do know what I am not.' He knew also what he was uniquely attempting: 'Your regard for me has at least awakened me to believe in the possibility that I may yet make some impression with my "light" – my "*dews*" – my "*breezes*" – my *bloom* and my *freshness* – no one of which qualities

46

have yet been perfected on the Canvas of any painter in the world.'

The thing which Constable did (and which most of us do not do) was to discover himself; and to leave behind him within the sarcasms, the unfairnesses, the doubts, the weaknesses, and the compromises, monuments of that discovery in the best of his paintings. Probably now his art is less in favour and less influential than it has been for the last fifty years. Constable comes late in a long phase of painting, of 'naturalism', which begins in the Renaissance with such artists as Uccello and is wearing out in our day when men are sickening of the representation of things as they appear to be. Yet it is always worth remembering that story of Blake and Constable, not only because it emphasizes the opposition between two conceptions of art (one of which is in some points much nearer the conception ruling in Europe today), but also because it warns us that Constable's art may not always be quite so literal as it seems. Looking at Constable's landscapes, you can do two things: you can see in their earth and trees, generalized yet naturally true, in their agitated clouds, their dropping rain, their light, and their disturbed freshness, more of value than they actually contain in the organization of the paint upon the canvas, because you realize Constable so much influenced European painting in the nineteenth century. The other thing is to see in Constable's paintings less of value than they contain because Constable was so personal an artist, whose art differs so much in its literalness from that of William Blake, for example. He did not look prosily at a landscape and transfer an accurate selection of it to

47

canvas. He was not a camera artist before the invention of the camera; but he projected his own emotions into the visible England of sky and cloud and light and vegetation; and so out of that visible England and his own emotions he made a painting literal up to a point, and limited to the painter. He did not believe in a painter's reality outside the material, visible world. In common with most painters, poets, novelists who came after him in the nineteenth century, he was a seeker after mortal moments who touches our hearts by showing his own. Blake wanted painters to seek after moments beyond mortality, as distinct from the mortal as diamond is distinct from flesh. In the National Gallery there is a large painting of a subject which Constable called 'Hadleigh Castle: The Mouth of the Thames – Morning after a Stormy Night'. On one side is the stump of a ruined castle. Below and across the picture stretches the agitated, wide estuary. But most of the picture, most of the paint in low, cool colours, goes to the sky, agitated again with broken clouds and birds tumbled and blown about. We know this picture was conceived and painted after one of the stormiest periods of night in Constable's life. His wife had died, leaving him agitated and alone with a large family of young children. He painted the picture in a high agony of nervous doubt over its success. Suppose we knew nothing of these circumstances, 'Hadleigh Castle' would still seem an agitated, personal, autobiographical picture, touching our hearts in that way. But where in a painting of the greatest masters can we deduce some mortal, agitated, pathetic moment in the life of the artist out of which the painting has arisen? That is the difference between the masterly arts of pathos and the great mastery, between mortal and immortal moments.

All the evidence of Constable's pictures and Constable's life and character shows that he felt the need to make something ordered, composed, and serene – something which he felt was tinged with immortality. Though he said that painting for him was only another word for feeling, many of his remarks suggest a wistful understanding of performances beyond such a conception. It was of paintings by Claude that he used the expression 'the calm sunshine of the heart'. He looked at a composition after Poussin (which is now in the National Gallery – No. 40 – and was the gift of Constable's unenthusiastic patron, Sir George Beaumont) and spoke of its grave morality. He was always after these moral feelings of landscape he spoke of in opposition to the shaggy satyrs of William Etty. He struggled, so he said, for 'sparkle with repose' in his pictures; and yet he felt himself so much 'employed' by the scenes he painted, so much employed, that is, by his own feelings embodied in the scene.

Blake once said about Wordsworth (deeper, more philosophical, serener, and more mature as a poet than Constable ever was as a painter) that he feared Wordsworth was too much in love with nature. As he looked over Constable's drawings he must have been certain that Constable was too much in love with nature; and then with surprise and relief he came upon that drawing of the fir-trees in which Constable passed beyond mere love of nature into something less mortal. He does not

D

do so often (perhaps his most diamond moments are achieved in some of the oil sketches of cloud scenery in the Victoria and Albert Museum), so we are left with those many paintings of the terrestrial scene which excite pity and sadness or those fresh, green, sparkling feelings of joy so closely knit with sadness. He said himself that his pictures were his 'acts': they are the acts indeed of a character honest and persistent, exultant and disturbed, joyful and melancholic, enjoying moments of serenity among the warmth and the asperities of human imperfection. We are rather moved by him than raised out of ourselves. Constable guarded his sensibility, and opened his heart only to nature, his canvases, and a few friends. He was a tender husband and a tender father to his children, loving in them, as he loved in nature, the exhilarating freshness of spring. He was extreme only in those detestations of all that seemed to interfere with the genuineness of painting. In religion he took a cautious middle way. He never allowed himself to worship nature, to be a pantheist, or to yield to excess. He put down that 'Our wisest and best teachers – the Seraphim themselves teach us – that our maker is most seen in his works – and best adored in our wonder and admiration of them'. That was enough. According to Leslie, he felt that 'the *supernatural* need not be the *unnatural*', and he cautioned one of his acquaintances 'against enthusiasm in religion, which, as it has no foundation, is apt to slip from under a man, and leave infidelity or madness'. Like many other remarkable artists, innovators in their own art, he was cautious politically as well – one thinks of Samuel Palmer and Degas or of Yeats and Mr T. S. Eliot. He was aristocratically inclined to reaction. Whereas his wild friend John Martin was a Reformer, the Reform Bill frightened Constable; and not only because he was worried about his finances. He wrote to Leslie: 'What makes me dread this tremendous attack on the constitution of the country is, that the wisest and best of the Lords are seriously and firmly objecting to it; and it goes to give the governement into the hands of the rabble and dregs of the people, and the devil's agents on earth, the agitators.'

Though Constable was narrow, the narrowness did not exclude depth. He mixed acid with sweetness; but it was the sweetness, as of a sound apple, which prevailed. His moderation kept his sensibility in order without deadening it. Far from being the country artist who painted clouds so accurately merely because his father had owned wind as well as water mills, he was scientifically curious and he interested himself in the meteorological science of his time. It is true that he had not the strength and the ruthlessness of the greatest practitioners. He compromised a little, but was still a lifelong devotee of his art, who was not mean, naïve, or ridiculous. And nothing was more wonderful in this man than his preserved belief in his own vision and methods, pressed upon as he was by uncomprehending fellow artists, uncomprehending patrons, and uncomprehending critics. He prepared his canvases and manipulated his paint with as much honesty as he felt and saw. Other painters in his time of romantic individualism rashly used unsafe grounds and risky ways of manipulation which gave their canvases a flashy and transitory splendour. Their pictures today are irretrievably blackened and cracked and flake away by the square inch. Constable's remain. He could say with the pride of humility, 'I have not to accuse myself of ever having prostituted the moral feeling of Art, but have always done my best.'

Flatford Mill, Suffolk

On the north bank of the River Stour, one mile south of East Bergholt. A group of buildings, typical of the district, comprising the mill, mill-house, and Willy Lott's cottage, all dating from the early seventeenth century. The cottage is a timber-framed structure, plastered and lime-washed. Its steep-pitched roofs are covered with dark red tiles made in the locality. There is no admission to the interiors of these buildings, which are not of architectural interest.

Hughenden Manor, HIGH WYCOMBE, BUCKINGHAMSHIRE

BENJAMIN DISRAELI

By I. R. Apt

' ... I trace all the blunders in my life to sacrificing my own opinion
to that of others. ... I have an unerring instinct – I can read characters
at a glance. ...'
'Poetry is the safety-valve of my Passions, but I wish to act what
I write.'

ARROGANCE, theatrical panache, and a confessed
love of poetry; few qualities could be less con-
genial to the English taste. To succeed with them in English public life, immense ability and charm would be
needed too. Yet the combination has succeeded with us
more than once, and may again – though never more
brilliantly than in the person of Benjamin Disraeli.

According to the astrologers, those born under Sagittarius have high ideals, a striking gift for being humor-
ous and entertaining, know well how to express their
opinions in public, but are too versatile and ambitious to
escape attacks of restlessness and deep depression. In one
instance, at any rate, they do not seem to have been far
out. Disraeli's birthday, 21st December 1804, makes him
a child of Sagittarius.

Both Benjamin's parents were middle-class Jews of
Italian origin. Isaac, his father, was a writer of essays who
had travelled much abroad and had kept up to date with
the ideas of his time. His mother took little part in her
children's education and does not appear to have had
much influence upon the character of her eldest son.

55

Doubtless the closest friend of Benjamin's childhood and adolescence was his sister Sarah, whom he affectionately called 'Sa'.

Though born to the Jewish faith, when Benjamin was twelve years old, all Isaac's children were baptised into the Church of England.

Young Benjamin Disraeli was educated at private schools where he acquired his first liking for the classics. When he was seventeen years old, he was articled to a firm of solicitors in Old Jewry, but felt extremely unhappy in his new work and surroundings. Eventually his health, never very strong, gave way, and the articles of service were cancelled. Then followed his first trip abroad, to the Netherlands and along the Rhine, which left a deep impression on him. Many years later he wrote, 'I determined, when descending those magical waters, that I would not be a lawyer'.

Meanwhile he had eagerly pursued his literary studies, and begun to go about socially. But to realize his ambitions, he needed money; and so involved himself in a scheme of speculations in South American shares. This resulted in large debts which were not finally settled till many years later. It is characteristic of Disraeli that instead of uselessly fretting and worrying about these financial difficulties, he immediately determined to write a book. Thus his first novel, *Vivian Grey*, was written before its author was twenty-one years old and published anonymously in 1826. It had a striking success. The hero, Vivian Grey, was transparently modelled upon Benjamin's own life and ambitions, his inner struggles, political aims, burning frustration, and unwavering belief in ultimate success. The author describes his hero's character early in the book: –

'For it was one of the first principles of Mr Vivian Grey that everything was possible. Men did fail in life, to be sure ... but still all these failures might be traced to a want of physical and mental courage ... so he had long come to the comfortable conclusion that it was impossible that his career could be anything but the most brilliant.'

The general tone of the book was sarcastic, the influence of Voltaire being clearly noticeable.

In the following year, Benjamin's health broke down again, and he went with some friends on another journey to Switzerland and Italy. The beautiful scenery deeply influenced his mind, and is sensitively portrayed in his later works.

During the next few years, Disraeli's health continued to be unstable, a fact which much depressed and discouraged him. His family had now moved to Bradenham in Buckinghamshire, and it was there that *The Young Duke* was written. This was a novel of fashion, its characters moving in exalted circles and revelling in luxury, extravagance, and splendour. The book was not a great success, but its proceeds enabled Benjamin to start off on an extended tour in the East – which had always particularly fascinated him – including Greece, Egypt, and Palestine. This journey strengthened his taste for the exotic, and gave him plenty of subject-matter for his next two novels, *Contarini Fleming* and *Alroy*.

By this time 'Dizzy' (as Mayfair had nicknamed him) had become a well-known figure in social and in minor political circles. It has been said that he 'pushed his way into public life by the force of acting'. The eccentricity of his dress, the theatrical entrance he made into a drawing-room, as though he were stepping on to a stage in full view of the audience, and the dramatic way in which he spoke, attracted immediate attention. His appearance was remarkable. Enormous rings sparkled on his white-gloved hands, his black curly hair glistened with pomade and smelt overpoweringly of scent. He would wear 'a satin waistcoat, frilled shirt, green or purple trousers with gold stripes, and the rest of his costume of like grotesqueness. He looked like a freak, but he talked like an oracle.' He himself wrote in his diary: –

'The world calls me *conceited*. The world is in error. ... When I was considered very conceited indeed I was nervous and had self-confidence only by fits. I intend in future to act entirely from my own impulse. ... My mind is a continental mind. It is a revolutionary mind. I am only truly great in action. If ever I am placed in a truly eminent position I shall prove this. I could rule the House of Commons, although there would be a great prejudice against me at first.'

By 1832 the Reform Bill struggle was at its height. It was at this point that Disraeli first began to devote himself seriously to politics, and replied to Lord Melbourne's indulgent inquiry as to what he would like to be, 'I want to be Prime Minister'. This was after he had been defeated twice in succession – at a bye-election in High Wycombe as a Radical candidate, and again at the general election of 1835. After this he threw in his lot with the Tories, contested a seat in a bye-election at

Taunton and sustained his third defeat. Early in 1836 *The Runnymede Letters* appeared, attacking Melbourne's Whig Government with bitter sarcasm. In the midst of all this political strife he found time to write two more novels: *Henrietta Temple*, a tender and touching love-story, and *Venetia*, which presents some of the chief episodes from the lives of Shelley and Byron.

In 1837 William IV died, and Victoria's reign began. Parliament was dissolved, a general election called, and Disraeli at last gained a seat as Conservative member for Maidstone. He was now thirty-two years old. His first speech in Parliament was anything but a success, but he kept on talking till his voice was drowned in general uproar, and concluded prophetically: 'I sit down now, but the time will come when you will hear me.' Sir Robert Peel was amongst the loudest to applaud him and warmly welcomed him to the Conservative ranks. Even so, 'Dizzy's' progress in politics was slow at first, and debts still hampered him.

Two years after his maiden speech, Disraeli got married. His first impressions of Mrs Wyndham Lewis, then wife of a Member of Parliament, were hardly complimentary. He had met her at a dinner-party a few years previously, and recounted the event in a letter to 'Sa': –

'I was introduced to Mrs Wyndham Lewis, a pretty little woman, a flirt, and a rattle; indeed gifted with a volubility I should think unequalled, and of which I can convey no idea. She told me that she liked "silent, melancholy men". I answered "that I had no doubt of it".'

Some time later, at the Rothschilds', his hostess asked

him: 'Mr Disraeli, will you take Mrs Wyndham Lewis in to dinner?'

'Oh, anything rather than that insufferable woman! However ... great is Allah!'

And he marched the 'insufferable woman' to dinner.

Soon after this incident Wyndham Lewis suddenly died, and Disraeli presently received a short but expressive note from a certain Count Alfred D'Orsay, who had won the position of a grand master of the dandies in London: –

'You will not make love! You will not intrigue! You have your seat; do not risk anything! If you meet a widow, then marry!'

It is doubtful whether this blunt counsel affected his decision, but Disraeli married Wyndham Lewis's widow, who was twelve years his senior, and moved into her house in Park Lane. They were ideally suited. Mary Anne, although somewhat ignorant and frivolous, understood men and knew how to take her husband. She admired him wholeheartedly, and made him feel that she only lived for him. Her frivolous talk amused and relaxed him, her tenderness lifted his spirits when he was assailed by one of his frequent moods of depression. He had found another Sarah, and a loving wife.

Disraeli's position in Parliament strengthened, his reputation grew, his literary achievements flourished. In 1844 he published one of his most powerful works, *Coningsby*, the first of a series of three political novels, and in the following year the second volume *Sybil*, which gives a moving picture of the pitiful condition of the working classes in the 'hungry forties', indirectly attacking the

Government's policies in general, and Peel's in particular. On the fly-leaf of *Sybil* were written the words: –

'I would inscribe these volumes to one whose noble spirit and gentle nature ever prompt her to sympathize with the suffering; to one whose sweet voice has often encouraged, and whose taste and judgement have ever guided their pages; the most severe of critics, but – a perfect wife!'

Stronger and stronger became his attacks on the Government, and when Peel resigned in 1846, Disraeli's victory came. He took his seat on the front opposition bench, now one of the principal men of his party. *Tancred*, the third volume of his political trilogy, was published at this time. It expresses his views on Eastern politics, about which he felt strongly, and the Jewish question. Of his own beliefs, Disraeli had never made any definite statement. He was interested in the principles of all the great religions, but had never received any definite instructions in either the Jewish or the Christian faith.

Victories now followed in quick succession. 1849 saw him as leader of the Conservatives in the Commons; two years later he was appointed Derby's Chancellor of the Exchequer, and at the same time became leader of the House of Commons. He had meanwhile lost his father and come into the possession of Hughenden Manor, near Beaconsfield. Here his deep love for the peace of the countryside, his yearning for simple country pleasures found full outlet. He assumed with relish the career of a country squire, but not at the expense of his social life, for he was now a well-known figure at Court and had attracted the attention of the Queen herself.

When, early in 1855, Aberdeen's Cabinet was compelled to resign, Palmerston formed a new Government, and after the general election two years later, the Whig party was well established. Palmerston died in 1865, Lord Derby became Prime Minister for the third time in succession, and Disraeli – whose reputation as a skilled statesman had spread rapidly – was at his side to help and support him. So no one was greatly surprised that when Derby was forced to retire through ill-health Disraeli took his place. Thus, at the age of sixty-three, his life's ambition was fulfilled at last. 'Yes,' he said, 'I have climbed to the top of the greasy pole.' However, the greasy pole was too slippery: difficulties soon arose, the new Prime Minister considered it necessary to dissolve his Parliament, the Liberals were returned with a vast majority, and Disraeli resigned, to be succeeded by Gladstone.

The chance of a rest was not wholly a misfortune, for his health had been weakening again. He returned to his country house, and in 1870 published *Lothair*, a satire on English Society. This had an enormous success.

Two years later Mary Anne died of cancer of the stomach. Disraeli was heartbroken. Indeed, his political friends feared that he might retire completely. But the opposite happened: to escape torturing memories and loneliness, he feverishly sought activity, resumed the battle with redoubled strength, and when Gladstone resigned in 1874, Disraeli became Prime Minister once more. The Queen welcomed his return with obvious delight, and so, with a strong majority behind him, 'Dizzy' held in his hands at last what he had longed for all his life: undisputed power. At last he had the inner satisfaction of knowing that he would be accepted for what he was. At last his mind could relax. His wit became less harsh, his sarcasm softened; but clouds of deep melancholy seemed to surround him. His *mots* had altered in tone: 'Are you quite well, Mr Disraeli?', friends would inquire. 'Nobody is quite well ...' was the laconic reply, and when at a social gathering he was asked what could be done to divert him, he would answer, 'Ah, let me exist!'

Doubtless his melancholy was caused to no small extent by his failing health, for he suffered from serious attacks of gout which greatly diminished his activity. He now devoted himself chiefly to a general supervision of the Government, and at the Queen's suggestion, went up to the House of Lords as Earl of Beaconsfield in 1876.

He had become a special favourite of the Queen, whom he called 'The Faery'. She opened her heart to him on all subjects; invited him everywhere; knowing his insatiable curiosity, she showed him her most secret correspondence; she even sent her own physician to his sick-room when he was confined to bed with another sharp attack of gout, and visited him personally. Seeing him so weak, she grew maternal and affectionate. The bond of friendship between them was a great comfort to both.

The remainder of Beaconsfield's life was mainly concerned with world politics, and especially with the Eastern question: the Bulgarian atrocities, the rout of Serbia, the Constantinople conference, and finally the Russo-

Turkish War. When the fighting stopped, Beaconsfield, accompanied by Salisbury who had taken over the Foreign Office, went to the Congress of Berlin as representatives of Great Britain. This was the zenith of his political career: his diplomacy and determination greatly impressed Bismarck. '*Der Alte Jude*,' he used to say, '*Das ist der Mann*.' ('The old Jew, that is the Man.') Beaconsfield got Cyprus and nearly all he wanted for England, and returned with Salisbury in a blaze of triumph, bringing home with him 'peace with honour'.

It was his last triumph. At the general election in 1880, the Liberals were returned to power, Gladstone again took the field, and on 21 April Beaconsfield finally resigned his office.

He accepted defeat with an inner peace of mind. At last he would be able to enjoy a little time of rest and complete relaxation amongst his trees in the country. His only sorrows were having to relinquish State affairs to others when great political problems were to hand, and the inevitable parting from the Queen. The farewell audience was a sad one; the Queen made him promise to come and visit her from time to time, a promise which he kept faithfully.

Throughout his whole life Disraeli had, in rhythmical waves, passed on from ambition to action, and from action to creation. Even now, though his body was weak, ill, and tired, his mind drove him on.

'When I want to read a novel,' he used to say, 'I write one.' And so he wrote his last book, *Endymion*, the story of a young politician who found success through the aid of friendships with women. This novel was welcomed

64

enthusiastically by the public, but had less financial success than *Lothair*.

It was his final creation. In March 1881 his gout worsened, attacks of asthma tortured him, and on 19th April he died.

His death was deeply mourned by millions. On the coffin were two wreaths from the Queen, one, of fresh primroses, with the inscription, 'His favourite flower'. On the other was a note written by the Queen's own hand: 'A token of true affection, friendship, and respect.' He was laid to rest at Hughenden, in the peace of the green countryside of which he had been so passionately fond.

The passing of centuries may obscure memories of Lord Beaconsfield's political successes; but the character of 'Dizzy' is too vivid ever to be forgotten: a man whose behaviour was unfailingly fascinating and dramatic, whose mental processes were as unusual as his looks, complex, sophisticated, simple, loving children and flowers and country things, an artist and statesman whose outward flourishes sprang from a deep understanding of his fellow men.

Hughenden Manor, Buckinghamshire

One and a half miles north of High Wycombe on the Great Missenden road. Bought by Disraeli in 1847 and transformed by him in 1862 into a red-brick Victorian mansion, with Gothic architectural trimmings. The interior is a museum, and the statesman's study is preserved exactly as he used it before his death in 1881.

E

THOMAS HARDY

By L. A. G. Strong

For many writers the place where they live is simply the place where they live. It has no effect upon their work, beyond that which arises from making them comfortable or uncomfortable while they are working. You would not know, from reading their books or plays, whether they lived at Chichester or Clacton. Hardy's work grew out of the place where he lived. It belonged to his Wessex; and, wherever he went and whatever he wrote about, he remained a countryman.

This was a cardinal fact about Hardy. He was part of a whole, never detached from that whole, never thinking, much less seeking, to transplant himself into a different environment. Those critics who acknowledge that he remained a countryman and at the same time complain of his use of the so-called pathetic fallacy, have I think missed an essential point about him. The pathetic fallacy puts man in the centre of the picture and makes nature subscribe to his mood. Urban critics, observing that a passionate scene between characters coincides with a thunderstorm, or that the heroine's gloom is accompanied by lowering skies, accuse the novelist of sentimentally subordinating the weather to the emotional temperature of his story. But Hardy's practice had a deeper source. For him, man and scene are parts of a whole. A movement of life was manifest in that part of the

66

Hardy's Cottage, HIGHER BOCKHAMPTON, DORSET

universe which he happened to be describing, through the sky and trees and stones no less than through the man. The writer, being a man, must emphasise the man's part in the whole, if only because human perceptions are the point of focus. If tree or stone were self-conscious, and could communicate, they would doubtless emphasise the viewpoint of tree and stone. So Hardy has, necessarily, a slight prejudice in favour of humankind. But it is only a slight prejudice. No major novelist whom I have read has less. He would have at once endorsed Robert Frost's poem in which the two lovers on the mountain side are confronted first by a doe, then by a buck : –

> Two had seen two, whichever side you spoke from.

Even though the poet must speak from the man's side, he has no more bias than his situation entails. He looks at the scene as a whole. Frost sees that life speaks sometimes harmoniously through several mouthpieces at once. In his poem he knows less about the minds of the deer than about those of the human lovers, because he is a man; but he acknowledges the deers' viewpoint, he respects their integrity, he does not regard them as properties of the scene. They are not a contrived or even a fortuitous encouragement to the lovers' mood. Lovers and deer, mountain and wall are balanced and partial expressions of something which means most to the lovers, because they can reflect on it and, in the end, perhaps understand it : –

> Still they stood,
> A great wave from it going over them,
> As if the earth in one unlooked-for favour
> Had made them certain earth returned their love.

In the same way Hardy and his home and his work were parts of a whole, the emphasis falling on Hardy because he was the point of consciousness, the medium through which the harmony found expression in words. His business was to understand and to communicate. I am labouring this point because it has been overlooked. Hardy, a writer of genius, was a product and a part of the region where he lived and about which he wrote. His solidarity, his unity of substance with it, was the source of his qualities, of all that is excellent in his work and all that is odd and even absurd. Bird-sharp eye, compassionate heart, a judgement at once uncorrupted and uninformed by urban civilization; all his qualities as a writer spring from his indissoluble unity with his background, and with them the paradoxes of vision, thought, and utterance that have perplexed so many readers and seemed to be contradictions, rather than consequences of the impact of three thousand years of European civilization upon a mind which never left its home. Hardy's days in London, his travels, his reading never changed the fabric or the temper of his mind. They merely gave it more to contemplate. He remained an original; a west-country original; from the point of view of cosmopolitan literature, an aboriginal. The French term *un originel*, carrying as it does a strong suggestion of oddity, expresses perfectly Hardy's relationship to the culture which France typifies, the polite world of European literature: and his advent into it had the shock, the grandeur and inconvenience of a south-westerly gale.

These originals – English literature is strong in them – have always an irreconcilable, unteachable side to their genius. The defect of their quality, the obverse side of their integrity, it can often hold them back and prevent them from being more than gifted oddities. Hardy's genius was so powerful that it swept his ineptitudes with it, like logs in a river; but they could sometimes cause hold-ups and momentarily disfigure the stream. The uncouth diction of some of his poems, the lumbering honesty of phrase, the eccentricities of grammar, the words and expressions which no form or rhythm could assimilate; the occasional inappropriateness of structure to material, the forcing of character to fit theme; the novelettish unreality of his high-life figures, his *nobles dames*; the ludicrous episode in *A Laodicean* where de Stancy falls in love with Paula through spying on her as she exercises in pink flannel underclothes, the critical standard which allowed him to praise *The Odyssey* as 'quite in the *Marmion* class' – these and a score of similar ineptitudes are the awkward reactions of a man whose imagination was in tune only with those realities which country life made manifest. Hardy's sense of reality was focussed on country things. Beyond that range, its light was uncertain, smoky, monstrous, or absurd. His country folk talk beautifully, every word rounded with conviction. Not so Sue Bridehead, Mrs Charmand, or Lady Mabella.

It is, I think, important to realize that, while these *gaffes* in Hardy rise from a defect in his imagination, that defect is in fact a part of his integrity, his unity with the rustic scene. In his work, the absurd and the sublime come from the same source. To realize this is to understand why he can at one moment be so little biased in favour of humanity, and at the next be angrily arraigning Providence for its indifference to man's welfare. The mystics who receive a vision of harmony in the universe are soon confronted with its cruel opposite. Some, like A.E., 'seek on earth what they have found in Heaven'. Others, with Housman, rail against 'whatever brute or blackguard made the world'. Hardy's primary apprehension seized upon the spectacle of man in harmony with nature, an obedient actor in the pageant of seedtime and harvest and the changing seasons. But that slow cyclic process brought its pains and its bewilderments. Even the unspeculative ploughman must be aware of storm and flood, of jealousy and bereavement, of the rabbit's squeal and the lamb's eyes pecked out by the crow. Nature is amoral, and man, a moral being, seems to think himself further and further out of tune with her. When first she scared him with her thunderstorms, her waterspouts, and her eclipses, he looked for gods to protect him. Once he had found them, it could not be long till he reproached them. They must control nature: what else would be the sense of praying to them for protection? Soon, they had created nature, and so were responsible for all she did. Why then do they suffer her so to mistreat her children? So it comes about that

> A stern voice asks the Immortals why
> They should plague us so.

Hardy has seen life manifest in a momentary harmony of man with cloud and stone and tree. He sees everywhere the universe groaning in travail. Projecting the conflict outwards, he throws the blame on an outside Force, and proceeds to blacken its name by an assemblage of mistakes, cross-purposes, and dire mischance unequalled since the plays of Webster, Ford, and Tourneur, and less plausible, since they are shown as operating from outside. Not the characters' own weaknesses, but some malignant outer power is at work, like a boy poking a stick into a bowl of goldfish.

That Hardy was obsessed by the idea of a governing power is shown throughout his work. He found confirmation of it in Greek tragedy, where the characters cannot escape their doom, and the extent of their free-will lies in the dignity with which they meet it. His Cornish tragedy explores the idea, *The Dynasts* embodies it. The conscientious, obsessive gloom of *Jude*, the hapless coincidences of *The Return of the Native*, all those tosses of the penny that so implacably come down tails, are the indignant projections upon the President of the Immortals of a countryman's discovery that the sentient part of the life-force has been forced disastrously out of tune. Which is the anomaly – man, or the universe? The question is too big; man, perplexed and anguished, uses the perceptions and the judgement he has been given, holds an enquiry, and brings in a verdict against his Creator.

This might as well be the conclusion of a city-dweller as of a countryman, but for two facts. The city-dweller has no first-hand evidence of harmony in nature. If he achieves unity with his background, it is with something which he and his forbears have made. The countryman's background is the earth ruled by the seasons, a world of weather and natural things. Besides, there is, it is important to remember, no element of sophistication in Hardy's thinking. He met such qualities of thought too late to understand, let alone be influenced by them. Just as on his visits to London and to famous houses he remained the countryman, with unconscious obstinacy failing to understand the well born, well educated people whom later in all honesty he tried to write about, so he never came to terms with the main current of European thought, and continued to make his rustic judgements, ranging from magnificence to absurdity, rooted always in the country his imagination could never leave. Thus inspiration with him often surpassed form, matter was stronger and more important than manner, and personality swept away design or virtually did without it.

All this might appear to suggest a bucolic genius, ill educated and in oafish isolation from cities and the world of letters. The world knows Hardy to be no such man. What it does mean is that this great descendant of the Dorset Hardys, though he came to London as a young man to study architecture, and was soon writing in letters to his sister shrewd comments on the fashionable novelist Thackeray, saw London always as a stranger, and, far from outgrowing Stinsford and Bockhampton, was confirmed in his loyalty to them. The crowds of London scared him: he lost his buttons in one, and could have lost his life, for six people were crushed and trampled to death close by. Soon, through that mysterious process of attraction whereby people meet the experiences appropriate to their nature, he was supervising the removal of coffins and skeletons as the Midland Railway drove a cutting through Old St Pancras Churchyard, and in one coffin found a skeleton with two skulls.

Religion called for the scrutiny of one who as a boy had dutifully sung in Stinsford choir.

'July 2 (1865). Worked at J. H. Newman's *Apologia*, which we have all been talking about lately. A great desire to be convinced by him, because Moule likes him so much. Style charming, and his logic really human, being based not on syllogisms but on converging probabilities. Only – and here comes the fatal catastrophe – there is no first link to his excellent chain of reasoning, and down you come headlong ...'

This – Hardy was twenty-two when he wrote it in his journal – is not the language of a yokel or of an innocent. Nor is this: –

'Patience is the union of moral courage with physical cowardice.'

Nor this: –

'The poetry of a scene varies with the minds of the perceivers. Indeed, it does not lie in the scene at all.'

Yet in those three entries we get much of the essential Hardy – lovable, shrewd, imaginative, honest, practical, and already set firmly within the limits of his genius. From the first, he had *authority*, that inner quality which may take years to emerge, but which the sensitive can discover even in a child. It comes from the depths: and it was in his depths that Hardy remained a countryman, a perceiver who was inalienably a part of the scene he perceived, and of the poetry which, however much he declared it to be a human gloss, he could never abstract from its manifestation. In the same way, he soon resolved to shut his mind against partiality and subservience to the views of others: –

'In future I am not going to praise things because the accumulated remarks of ages say they are great and good, if those accumulated remarks are not based on observation. And I am not going to condemn things because a pile of accepted reviews ... say antecedently that they are bad.'

A cure for despair was to read, not Wordsworth's immortality *Ode*, but his *Resolution and Independence*: and we find Hardy shrewdly insuring himself as a creative artist against his own limitations: 'A widely appreciative mind mostly fails to achieve a great work from pure far-sightedness.' The man who so early settled down in his native Dorset with his first wife had resolved not to let the cultured world upset his views or modify his opinions. The resolve held, strengthened by the attacks upon his novels and the idiotic revisions suggested by editors. Everything converged to deepen his sense of isolation from London and to justify him in the position he had never really quitted in his most pliable years. Thus we find him in 1915 criticising Bergson in almost the same terms as he had used of Newman fifty years before: –

'His theories are much pleasanter ones than those they contest, and I for one would gladly believe them; but I cannot help feeling all the time that his is rather an imaginative and poetical mind than a reasoner's, and that for his charming and attractive assertions he does not adduce any proofs whatever.'

Hardy's own imaginative and poetical mind demanded of the philosopher the qualities he supposed that he himself possessed; and for his own terrifying and embittered assertions, his consistent violation of the laws of probability so that caprice and mischance should bedevil the fortunes of Eustacia and Jude and Tess and many another, he adduced no proof, nor could he even claim, within the terms of his own programme, that they were based on observation.

One more quotation, from the same letter: –

'You must not think me a hard-headed rationalist for all this. Half my time – particularly when writing verse – I "believe" (in the modern sense of the word) not only in the things Bergson believes in, but in spectres, mysterious voices, intuitions, omens, dreams, haunted places, etc., etc. But I do not believe in them in the old sense any more for that. ...'

The attractions of Bergson's *élan vital* for the novelist who sent Eustacia roaming in agony on Egdon Heath were immediate and obvious: but the mind at rest, the mind unkindled, kept its market-day shrewdness and would not commit itself 'any more for that'. The kindled mind, at work in poetry, could believe and feel uncritically. 'I hold that the mission of poetry is to record impressions, not convictions.' And – an entry revealing his awareness of how little he had changed in his depths :–

'I believe it would be said by people who knew me well that I have a faculty (possibly not uncommon) for burying an emotion in my heart or brain for forty years, and exhuming it at the end of that time as fresh as when interred. ... Query: where was that sentiment hiding itself during more than forty years?'

At Dorchester, he might have answered; but he never pursued such questions far. 'I am not at all a critic.' Yet he liked to have his opinions confirmed. He said that *Il*

77

Trovatore was good music, and, the very next day – 4th November 1927 – proclaimed his pleasure at reading an article by Ethel Smyth, saying that *Il Trovatore* was good music. This humility, creating humility in others, disparaged a gift which would more than equip many a professed critic: –

'Thoughts on the recent school of novel-writers. They forget in their insistence on life, and nothing but life, in a plain slice, that a story *must be worth the telling*, that a good deal of life is not worth any such thing, and that they must not occupy a reader's time with what he can get at first hand anywhere around him.'

Sound, countryman's sense – needing only the proviso that the operative word is 'get'; for there are writers whose imagination can illumine what lies around us and reveal its meaning, where all we could see would be the outward circumstance.

Hardy was the greatest of English country writers, a novelist and poet of genius whose range was from the everyday detail of vernacular and seasonal ritual to the towering images of human destiny, magnificent as the pageantry of thunderclouds on a lurid sky, images thrown as it were on a huge screen dividing this world from the next, the boundary line between time and eternity. Yet at its most sublime, its angriest peaks, the idiom is earth-rooted; the bird-sharp eye of the countryman can focus lovingly on robin and snail or scan the indifferent heavens, and bring the same courage to both. To recall him is to think of the conversations of men in country inns, the slow music of their talk; to see the reddle on the sheep's fleece, the dark curve of Egdon, the

78

moon-cast shadows of Stonehenge; to hear the talk of the cliff watchers waiting for Bonaparte, and, looking up into the dark clouds above them, the thunderous murmur of those Powers whom the quiet man so passionately indicted. Little and big, he felt for them all. There is no writer whose house meant more to his life and writing, none therefore which his country should be at greater pains to keep as he left it.

Higher Bockhampton, Dorset

Three miles north-east of Dorchester, south of the Blandford road. A simple brick cottage with a thatched roof. The principal rooms are on view, but there are no relics of the author.

HENRY JAMES

By L. P. Hartley

I<small>T</small> was in 1897 that Henry James first came to live at Lamb House in Rye. He was fifty-four and had already been more or less settled in England for twenty years. The house offered, so he told his sister-in-law, Mrs William James, 'the solution of my long unassuaged desire for a calm retreat between May and November'. He took it on a long lease, but later bought it, and until he died in 1916 he spent most of his summers and a few of his winters there.

'I will try', he told his correspondent, 'to have a photograph taken of the pleasant little old world town-angle into which its nice old red-bricked front, its high old Georgian doorway and a most delightful little old architectural garden-house, perched alongside of it on its high brick garden-wall – into which all these features together so happily "compose".'

Here, at Lamb House, he had his friends to stay, but never more than two at a time. He seems to have been an anxious host, always uneasy about the quality of the food, but no doubt he was glad to return some of the hospitality he had received, for surely no man has ever been more greedily entertained than he was. No less than 108 times, he notes, he had dined out one winter; perhaps the time had come to put a stop to so much social distraction. Soon he gave up his flat in De Vere Gardens,

Lamb House, RYE, SUSSEX

F

and until 1912, when he took a flat in Carlyle Mansions, a room at the Reform Club was his only perch in London.

Lamb House was therefore the signal for a partial withdrawal from the social round which had meant so much to him, both of strain and pleasure. At Lamb House he could defend his privacy; until three o'clock in the afternoon he was inaccessible. But he did not shut himself up; he was incurably sociable. In Sussex he had literary neighbours, Joseph Conrad and H. G. Wells; but he also soon made friends with the townspeople of Rye. He attended tea-parties and became a familiar and respected figure. Though knowing little about flowers, he had an excellent gardener, and recorded his surprise and delight when, at a local flower-show, he discovered that a prize had been awarded to 'Mr James's carnations'. He was also a member of the golf-club. But, though he told someone that he chose Rye as a residence because he liked golfers in plus fours, he could not give the game itself his blessing. 'A princely expenditure of time', he called it on one occasion; and to E. F. Benson (his successor at Lamb House) he summarized it impressionistically as 'some beflagged jampots, my dear Fred, let into the soil at long but varying distances. A swoop, a swing, a flourish of steel, a dormy.'

The taking of Lamb House might be reckoned as a water-shed in Henry James's career. It intervened between two periods of his literary development: his early courtship of the theatre, which ended so disastrously with the failure of *Guy Domville* in 1895, and the third flowering of his genius for fiction: the complex novels of spiritual dilemma starting in 1901 with *The Sacred*

Fount. Roughly, it coincided with what some think the peak of his achievement; with the appearance of two of his best-loved novels, *The Spoils of Poynton* and *What Maisie Knew*; with what is perhaps the most popular of all his stories, *The Turn of the Screw*; and it preceded, by only two or three years, *The Awkward Age*, that dazzling and entertaining transition-piece between his middle and his later manner, and the last novel perhaps in which his interest in his characters was at least equal to, if not greater than, his absorption in his theme.

His arrival at Lamb House also marked, according to Mr Percy Lubbock, what has been held to be an important change in his method of composition. Before, he had only made occasional use of dictation; now it became a habit – not only for his books but sometimes for his letters (he apologizes for their 'Remingtonese'). But how hard it is to arrive at the truth. Mr Simon Nowell-Smith, whose ingenious and delightful compilation, *The Legend of the Master*, has put every admirer of Henry James in his debt, makes amusing play with the conflicting evidence for when this habit of dictation was begun. Was it in 1885, when James was writing *The Princess Casamassima*? Challenged, the Master seems to have agreed that it was. But he also agreed with another interlocutor, who surmised that the change took place in 1896, when James was at work on *What Maisie Knew*. What are we to make of such discrepancies? One thing seems to emerge – that the habit of dictation cannot be held responsible for the inflation of James's later style, since neither external nor internal evidence can tell us at what point the habit began.

More important, perhaps, for the student of James's literary development is the fact that about this time he ceased to 'go behind' his characters, explaining each from the character's own point of view in the fashion of the great novelists of the past, and left them to explain themselves. If indeed it be a fact. Writing to Mrs Humphry Ward in 1899 he says, 'I "go behind" right and left in "The Princess Casamassima", "The Bostonians", "The Tragic Muse", just as I do the same but singly in "The American" and "Maisie", but just as I do it consistently *never at all* (save for a false and limited *appearance*, here and there, of doing it a *little*) ... in "The Awkward Age".'

If this is so – and we have it from the horse's mouth, not from a reporter – then the publication of *The Awkward Age* is a vital date not only in the history of Henry James's own development but in the history of English fiction. James may have had few direct imitators, but his influence – in this very matter of presenting his characters without explaining them – has been enormous, and can be traced in the work of almost every serious novelist of the present day – in Miss Elizabeth Bowen's no less than in Miss Compton-Burnett's. The modern novelist has renounced 'omniscience'; he does not comment or interpret, he leaves his characters to make their own impression and tell their own tale.

How far this renunciation of a privilege which, as James himself says, was automatically claimed by Dickens, Thackeray, Balzac, and Tolstoy, was a gain or a loss to fiction as a whole, is much too large a subject to enter into here. That it refines and strengthens the *art* of fiction, most people would agree. That it reduces the scope of the novel, and limits the novelist's interpretation of life, is also probably true. It all depends on whether a novel can be, or ought to be, a perfect work of art.

One sees how Henry James arrived at his theory. It was through his love of the theatre, his passion for drama. Fiction appeared to him to be essentially dramatic: 'Dramatize! Dramatize!' he would exclaim. Now, anything in the nature of an explanation is abhorrent, indeed destructive to drama – as witness the weakening effect of such devices as asides and even soliloquies. Everything must be inferred, nothing must be told. Hence Henry James's dislike of direct statement. 'How can you say I do anything so foul and abject as to state?' he asked Hugh Walpole. The consequence is that in his later work his characters exist chiefly in virtue of their relationship to each other, and to their general predicament, which the conclusion of the novel is to straighten out. He never completely dehumanized his characters: he had too strong a sense of and respect for personality to do that. But whereas Daisy Miller and Princess Casamassima are persons in their own right – we can think of them apart from their fictional context – the tormented quartet in 'The Golden Bowl' are almost like algebraic symbols in an equation or lines in a parallelogram of forces, so interdependent are they.

Henry James's later method came to exclude both the lyrical and the epical from fiction, and that is one reason why, perhaps, he so amazingly under-rated the novels of Thomas Hardy, which are full of both, and Meredith's. He could endure no relaxation of the dramatic tension –

anything that did not contribute to that must be kept out as irrelevant. He was an extremely severe critic of the work of some of his great contemporaries, though on the whole an indulgent one to the generation of novelists that was springing up. Progressively as he grew older did his conviction deepen that he himself was on the right track. The failure of his books to sell did not daunt him; he brushed aside criticism and complained of the thick wits of readers and reviewers when they complained of his obscurity. Nothing in all his writing is more moving than the passage in his private papers, meant for his own eye only, in which he welcomes the return of his genius. '... I seem to emerge from these recent bad days – the fruit of blind accident – and the prospect clears and flushes, and my poor blest old Genius pats me so admirably and lovingly on the back that I turn, I screw round, and bend my lips to passionately, in my gratitude, kiss its hands.'

What utter abandonment to passion makes itself felt in that tremendous split infinitive – the only passion, so far as we know, that Henry James gave way to in his life. Only perhaps in Emily Brontë's poem to her genius do we find the same explicit confidence in inspiration, and the feeling of what it means to whoever has it.

James was not the only novelist whose life was given to his art and who seems to have had no important emotional experience outside it. But surely no other novelist has dedicated himself to his art as completely and deliberately as he did. Lamb House was the temple – the shrine in which he worshipped it. There is no doubt that he

87

regarded art as a substitute for life, which was partly why he could not brook in fiction the untidiness and irrelevance of which life is full. Many great novelists, e.g. Tolstoy and Charlotte Brontë, have drawn largely on their own experiences for the material for their books; they have brought in their day-dreams too, making their art a vehicle for self-expression. It was not so in James's case. He may have identified himself to some extent with such young expatriated Americans as Strether and Ralph Touchett; but the germs of his stories came to him from outside in the form of 'situations', dramatic juxtapositions which had no bearing on his own life, but which he instinctively knew could be developed into a novel. And sometimes he would follow up an idea (as he does in *The Bench of Desolation*) almost without reference to its verisimilitude; he tested it by the canons of art, not by its likeness to life, his own or other people's.

Loneliness, so he told Logan Pearsall Smith, must be the artist's watchword. Inner loneliness, he must have meant, for no artist can ever have had more friends or been more sensitive to the obligations of friendship. Think of his letters, not only of their number and length, but of all the different people they were addressed to, with all of whom he was on the most affectionate terms, with all of whose special circumstances he was familiar enough to make the letter not merely an acknowledgement and a signal, but a personal communication. Often they were written in the small hours of the morning. Think of the devotion that all this extra mental effort implied, coming at the end of a hard day's work! And he

was as indefatigable a conversationalist as he was a correspondent. His verbal output of sociability must have
been as great as Dr Johnson's.

Yet even in his letters, and in his conversation, we see
his artistic conscience at work, correcting, editing, and
refining the activities of his social impulse. In all the letters it would be hard to find one carelessly written sentence. He wrote to his friend, yes; but in writing he took
care to satisfy that sleepless taskmaster whom it was, for
him, even more important to propitiate than the reci-
pient of the letter. And so in conversation, it was not so
much what he said that was important as the way he said
it; H. G. Wells's variously reported gibe about an elephant picking up a pea was true of his talk also. He talked
not so much *to* his interlocutor, as to give his interlocutor, and himself, a demonstration in the art of verbal expression. Hence his agonized search for the right word –
the word he owed to art, not to his audience – to
show that standards not only could but must be kept
up.

He was a slave to standards, and not only to artistic
but to moral and even to conventional standards. H. G.
Wells remarked how, on the hall table of Lamb House,
'lay a number of caps and hats, each with its appropriate
gloves and stick; a tweed cap and a stout stick for the
marsh, a soft comfortable deer-stalker if he were to turn
aside to the golf-club, a light felt hat and a cane for the
morning walk down to the harbour, a grey felt with a
black band and a gold headed cane of greater importance
if afternoon calling in the town was afoot.' He accepted
convention, and to some extent conventional opinion, as

an index and criterion of morality. This is most important, because if he was an artist first, he was a moralist second – indeed it would not be fanciful to say that his art was an aspect of his moral sense, so closely was it bound up with his feeling of obligation. In all his stories there is, if not a moral theme, a continual reference to moral judgement, sometimes delicate and almost flippant, as in *What Maisie Knew*; sometimes tantalizingly ambiguous, as in *The Ambassadors*; sometimes breathing fire and brimstone, as in *The Turn of the Screw*; and sometimes elevated to the most important thing in life, as in *The Golden Bowl*. The rules of morality might be as hard to find and as hard to practise as the rules of art, but they must be found and their workings illustrated. Nor were they to be found in defiance of public opinion. In this James differed from the master of his youth, Nathaniel Hawthorne, who accepted conventional society but questioned its moral judgements. Henry James would never have written a novel which seemed to mitigate the sin of adultery.

Born in New York, educated at Harvard, much travelled in Europe, in early life Henry James liked to call himself a cosmopolitan. By nature, and choice, he was intensely critical. Not long before his death, writes Mr Percy Lubbock, 'he confessed that at last he found himself too much exhausted for the "wear and tear" of discrimination; and the phrase indicates the strain upon him of the mere act of living'. He found the Americans of his time distressingly capable of vulgarity, and the English (especially in æsthetic matters) of stupidity. The English are the only people, he told his sister, 'who can do great things without being clever'. While the Continent, in spite of its attraction for a sophisticated mind, did not fulfil his exacting moral requirements. It was full of dubious noblemen intent on marrying guileless American heiresses. Of the three, though with more than one nostalgic glance at America, he chose England as a place to live in. The purchase of Lamb House was a sign that he had finally thrown in his lot with us, and as time went on he became steadily more English in feeling. The 1914 war accelerated the process of identification. He left Lamb House and took a flat in Chelsea, and remained there 'almost uninterruptedly till the end'. In June 1915 he took the step, criticized by some, of having himself naturalized an Englishman – though, said Mr Asquith, who acted as one of his sponsors, 'the bonds of friendship were strained to cracking when I had to subscribe to the proposition that he could both talk and write English'. He threw himself heart and soul into the war, talking to soldiers, interesting himself in Belgian refugees, and helping in every way he could. His faculty of writing, far from being paralysed by happenings so foreign to the natural tenor of his mind, was enormously stimulated. He began a new book of reminiscences; he wrote an introduction to Rupert Brooke's *Letters from America*. Only his creative imagination could not breathe the war atmosphere, and he abandoned the contemporary scene for 'The Sense of the Past'.

Just before his death, Edmund Gosse brought him the news that he had been awarded the O.M. Lying with closed eyes he made no sign of having heard, and Gosse tiptoed away, leaving the room to the patient, the nurse, and the light of a single candle. But the moment the door closed James opened his eyes and said, 'Nurse, take away the candle and spare my blushes'. He had paid England the highest compliment he could, and England had returned it.

Lamb House, Sussex

In West Street, Rye. An attractive eighteenth-century brick house, in which Henry James lived from 1897 to 1916. His study is arranged as a museum, with his furniture, pictures, books and other relics.

Batemans, BURWASH, SUSSEX

RUDYARD KIPLING

By Hilton Brown

❖

BATEMANS, BURWASH, SUSSEX, is an old stone-built house with old long-tended gardens; dignified, patrician, and correct; essentially English. Like most old houses, it has had its ups and downs, its peaks and depressions, but it may long regard as the apex of its fame the years when it was the property and residence of Rudyard Kipling. Kipling achieved Batemans late in life and after tribulation; he cast himself, within its walls, in the role of Sussex gentleman-farmer, prize herd of cattle and all; he cherished it warmly for two decades; he would have wished – though this was denied him – to die in it.

When he took over Batemans, Kipling was thirty-seven, enormously celebrated (though not quite so celebrated as he had been), a man who had seen the world in more senses than one. Short and neatly-made, he had settled physically into his final lines, and his face had assumed the shape it was to wear without structural alteration till his death thirty years later. Its conspicuous features were the formidable chin beneath the equally formidable moustache, the bright penetrating eyes behind the powerful lenses, and the darkness or duskiness of complexion that had led to the unkind, untrue, and totally unsustainable assertion that he had Indian blood in his veins. It was a face stamped by character and experience, though it was less attractive – and much less serene – than might have been expected from photographs of the handsome little boy he had been thirty years earlier. He affected unbecoming cloth caps of rather overwhelming dimensions, but otherwise his dress was normal. He looked intelligent, wary, and resolute. He was quiet and reserved; he liked to sit back and watch. He was affable but not effusive; he knew what he wanted and he meant to get it. He brought with him to Batemans an American wife even smaller than himself and two children, a boy and a girl, of the school-going age. He was well off but careful with his money. His health had been shattered by a recent illness in America and he preferred to spend his winters abroad; he was also, at the time of his arrival in Sussex, recovering slowly from a series of domestic disasters. So much the inquiring neighbours at Batemans could find out – and doubtless did find out – for themselves. But they must have said to one another, 'Here is a façade neither repellent nor wholly prepossessing; what sort of man lies hidden behind it?' It was not an altogether easy question to answer.

For a character portrait of Kipling at any period of his life it is necessary to remember one cardinal fact: he had suffered from the most disastrous form of childhood – that which opens with every indulgence and is suddenly plunged into abject misery. And for the Kipling who came to Batemans it is necessary to remember also that at the height of his power and the summit of his reputation he had been struck down by what was very nearly a mortal illness and at the same time had lost his eldest child, the beautiful little Josephine, who was – to judge by what he has written – his dearest creature. In the years before his coming to Batemans, Kipling had been through the Valley. From these disasters had arisen that sudden change in his character and his writings which has so needlessly surprised many of his admirers and so delighted most of his detractors. Surprise or delight, nothing more clearly discovers the shallowness of most estimates of Kipling. A man who has been brought to the gates of death and has seen his dearest possession pass through them can hardly continue precisely as before. Kipling was inevitably driven into that introspection for which the betrayal of his childhood had prepared him; throughout the Batemans period of his life he was sinking deeper and deeper into it, and he remained immersed in it till his death. Hence the mysticism and 'obscurity' of so much of his later work and that preoccupation with odd mental and bodily states that has puzzled so many of his readers. The ill-starred American adventure of 1892–9 broke Kipling's life so completely into two that the Kipling of the latter half, the Kipling of Batemans, is almost unrecognizable as the Kipling of the former.

In a portrait of this kind it is unnecessary to enter into elaborate biographical detail, but there are one or two items which must be mentioned because of their formative influence on Kipling's character. In the first place, he was the offspring on both sides, his father's and his mother's, of a protestant and proselytizing sect of Christianity. The Kipling and Macdonald ancestors were preachers, men with a mission, wearing the mantles of prophets, men very certain of their beliefs and very

G

assured in their exposition. In his bones Kipling was just such another. Time and again in his writings is expressed his eager admiration for the man who *knew* and his readiness to cast himself in that not always attractive role. So much so that when he lacked exact knowledge he must assume it; he must garner technicalities and lead them out like trump cards – or he must just boldly and straightforwardly bluff. This came the more easily to him because he did not in fact seek knowledge in the scholar's sense; his opinion was readily – too readily – made up on any topic that might confront him, social, political, or metaphysical, and, once made up, it hardened into an article of faith and was not allowed to alter. For this assurance in his beliefs and desire to proclaim, even to over-proclaim them, his Methodist ancestry may well be responsible.

Another corollary of his circumstances was that his mind should be turned to imperial ideas. Kipling was born in India at a time when British supremacy seemed unquestioned and almost unquestionable. The Mutiny was quelled, the Indian Congress was still far from its birth; it was an era when the Sahib was a Sahib indeed. For the first five years of his life no suggestion can have been made to his mind from any quarter that the British were not a dominating, imperial, and 'heaven-born' race. And when he came back to India and the *Civil and Military Gazette* twelve years afterwards – it was only twelve years afterwards – that was the impression that stuck. He refused to see – as, with his gifts of sympathy and observation, he must have been able to see – what was coming; he took his India, as he took so many things, at face value, summed it up and was done with it. The charm and beauty of his mother and the genius rather than the official position of his father introduced the Kipling family into Viceregal circles; the Commander-in-Chief was a familiar figure; the Indian Army Officer of the eighties, that resplendent and conquering demigod, was Kipling's companion and became his ideal. The voyage to England and back had taught him that the globe was a small place; presently, from a more ambitious expedition, he learned that the British Empire was a chain enclosing and linking – and fettering? – the world. It was also, he thought, and should be, an imperishable heritage for his countrymen. With what disgust would he survey the detractors and discarders of the Empire today – and how right in many ways he would be. For – this must be made clear – his 'Imperialism' which has horrified so many virtuous persons was not the Nazi craving for domination for its own sake; he sincerely believed – what is in fact substantially true – that the British had a mission and a duty to their 'new-caught sullen peoples', that British rule and governance, handled and administered as it was by the elite of creation, was the best thing for these peoples that had ever happened to them. Why then should it not be perpetuated for ever? It was one of the fundamental limitations of Kipling's character that he did not believe in change and was persuaded that it need not occur; he never seems to have asked himself what should happen if and when the Indian or African, or whoever the new-caught and sullen might be, decided that British rule and governance, however estimable, had lasted long enough. He does not even seem to have

supposed that such a question could ever arise. To be incapable of following an idea to its logical conclusion is a
complementary weakness of those with dogmatic and
readily acquired opinions; it was so with Kipling.
With his upbringing and antecedents he could not but
believe in the Empire but he never made any real attempt to think out the implications of the Imperial idea;
it was for him a plain and stable fact of existence and
those who thought otherwise were fools or knaves.
Thereby he provided his enemies with a powerful wea-
pon – and powerfully indeed have they used it.

Let us now look back again to that aspect with which
we started, Kipling's childhood. Born in India, he spent
the first five years of his life there, as thoroughly spoilt
and coddled no doubt as any other Anglo-Indian child;
it must be common knowledge that at the end of that
time his parents, bowing to the well-meaning but
misguided convention that has caused so much grief in
Anglo-Indian families, decided that their boy could not
safely remain longer in the East. They accordingly took
him home with his younger sister and boarded the pair
with certain persons in Southsea, a retired naval officer
of sorts and his wife. These were not, as they are often
misrepresented, relations but merely people who undertook the care of children in similar circumstances to the
Kiplings'. In *Baa Baa Black Sheep* Kipling has told the
hideous sequel; it need not, indeed cannot, be embel-
lished. The woman in whose charge Ruddy and Trix
had been left was a sadist and her son was another; Kipling at five was a spoilt and rowdy child, no doubt with
that boisterous humour he so enjoyed as an adult; the

clash was inevitable and the resulting horrors. We need not dwell upon these; what interests us here is the effect of those terrible years on Kipling's character.

They gave him in the first place a complete distrust in humanity, a determination to rely on himself alone, to be independent, to 'own oneself', never again to let oneself be subjected to such indignities and obstructions. It became necessary to succeed, to succeed tremendously and profitably, if only for that reason. They gave him further a canniness towards life and its promises; he was not to be gulled again by what looked like a fair and enticing prospect; henceforward he would look at both sides of Fate's penny. They inspired in him a sympathy with the under dog, the persecuted or unappreciated – for example, the British Tommy. Yet at the same time they hardened him. There must always have been a strain of roughness in his character, derived perhaps from some Yorkshire ancestor; under the Southsea regime this developed into downright callousness. There is no doubt that Kipling *enjoyed* the dog-fights he brings into the Mulvaney stories, the beatings and killings, the Bertrams and Bimis, even the horrors of the Chicago canning-factories he described with such gusto. But in condemning his delight in brutality for brutality's sake, the years of torment at Southsea must be taken into account; it was a quality partly ingrained and born in him but partly also developed as a carapace against ill-treatment. For many years he played it up assiduously, though by the Batemans period a kinder world had driven it into abeyance.

It is just possible also that the ostracism and

101

humiliations of Southsea worked upon another fundamental trait of Kipling's character – the desire to attach
himself to someone, to *belong*. All his life he had a passion to render himself the initiate, one of a brotherhood,
a hierarch with special knowledge, no matter of what;
and though much of this was his longing to be 'in the
know', some of it may have been sheer loneliness. He
almost necessarily became a Freemason, though having
become one he did not trouble to go much farther in the
Craft. His best long book is about a disciple, Kim, and
a lama teacher – to Kipling almost an ideal relationship.
To be the man who knew the answers, whether to a
ritual litany, a technical problem or merely to the simple
question 'How does it work?', that was always his dearest ambition. He could be the eternal Scoutmaster ex-
pounding round the camp-fire to attentive Scouts and
Guides, or failing that he could be one of the admiring
circle. But a circle of some kind was a necessity to him
and perhaps this may date from the Black Sheep experiences. Perhaps sometimes at Southsea, outcast and alone,
he thought how nice it would be to be one of a family,
like that of his Burne-Jones cousins; how delightful it
certainly was to visit them and be absorbed into their
Arabian Night or Scandinavian clubs. A club, a society,
a guild, a brotherhood – these were things for which he
craved. And yet – here was a conflict he could never resolve – this jarred continually with his other elementary
instinct to keep himself to himself. 'He travels the fast-
est' ... that was a canon in his creed. It was a conflict between brotherhood and privacy which kept him always
at arm's length from his fellows, always a hedgehog,

prickly and ready to curl into an impregnable ball, always a little difficult, prone to snub harshly and ruthlessly those who sought to rush him or trespass on his ring-fenced ground. One can see very clearly throughout his work how these contrary determinations vexed him, how uneasy and uncomfortable they made him, how they could render him excellent company at one moment and in one mood, and almost unapproachable in the next. It may explain also why he was so often at his best with children; you can open yourself to children without fear of advantage being taken, and when children begin to be tiresome you can send them away.

To charge Kipling with insincerity or 'inconsistency', as did the puzzled critics of the 'nineties, is to talk nonsense; he was a writer of fiction, inspired by an imagination so vivid that he became for the time being the character of whom or in which he wrote. It is equally short-sighted – though this time there is a better excuse – to call him conceited. Quite clearly he regarded himself from childhood onwards – and of course with perfect justification – as a superior being; it was simply a fact; God had made him so, and he could be gravely and pettily annoyed when others failed to recognize it. Few of us, endowed with Kipling's genius, would probably feel otherwise. Yet naturally this was not always appreciated, and the irritating know-all manner of his earlier writing did little to help. He must have infuriated his schoolfellows at Westward Ho! by his calm contempt of their groundling activities; he infuriated similarly a great many people in India and in Vermont and in literary London. Yet when he protested that he was but a tool in the hands of his 'daemon', that his work was but a stumbling effort to translate the promptings of the Divinity he dimly apprehended and reverently adored, he was perfectly sincere. Conscious of superiority, he was never pleased with himself. Nor had he the pretentious tyro's belief in his inspiration; work, solid work, he held, was the only thing that produced results, and to this principle he diligently devoted his practice.

Persons who have seen Kipling at Batemans have described him as a small shrinking figure scuttling, almost bolting, for the Downs in the company of a dog. There was perhaps something symbolic in that solitary tramping fugitive. All genius is lonely; it is one of the penalties adhering to the gift; but one cannot avoid the impression that Kipling was, even for a genius, an exceptionally lonely man. The strong man standing alone was no doubt often his ideal but as often it was an ideal betrayed by that contrary urge to be accepted in a band or body of his peers. Yet as soon as he took a step in that direction, he took a longer step back; as soon as he attracted, he repelled. His intimacies were extraordinarily few. And it was yet another of the misfortunes of his life that the one family outside his own relations which seemed ready to draw him into its bosom involved him in disappointment and indeed in tragedy.

The entry of the Balestiers of Brattleboro, Vermont, into Kipling's life was most certainly a milestone in it; it is interesting to speculate what might have happened to Kipling if Wolcott Balestier had not come to London at the beginning of the 'nineties. Wolcott was a publisher or publisher's agent and was concerned to make contacts; a necessary contact in those days was Gosse and Gosse as inevitably sent Wolcott to Kipling. Kipling fell for him with a rapidity and thoroughness which have puzzled all subsequent beholders, for there is no evidence that Wolcott Balestier was other than meritoriously commonplace. Yet Kipling wrote of him as of a demigod. Wolcott's influence might have faded, but he brought with him to London his sister Caroline, and in 1892 Carrie acquired Kipling – there is really no other word for it – as a permanent possession. The sequel was natural; when a financial crash cut short their world-tour honeymoon, nothing was more suitable than for the newly married pair to start a fresh life among the Balestier antecedents in Vermont. This was not, as often represented, a holiday visit; it was a migration. But alas! it was doomed. Wolcott Balestier had died but there remained at Brattleboro the other brother Beattie and in four years Beattie's quarrel with Kipling hounded the Kiplings out of America for good. It was a pity. I have it on very good authority that Beattie liked Kipling and Kipling liked Beattie (he was predisposed to like *any* Balestier) and the settlement with the in-laws in Vermont seemed to open under the most propitious auspices. Beattie was no doubt a 'character', an odd fish and wayward; but Kipling had no objection to characters, he was wayward himself and the odder the fish the more welcome to his net. Both Kipling and Beattie regretted the quarrel, as Beattie at least subsequently admitted. Yet it was mortal. The causes of it have been variously stated, but from such trustworthy authority as can be obtained, it would seem that much of the blame must rest on

Carrie, Mrs Kipling. Beattie was building a house for the Kiplings, the celebrated 'Naulakha', and it is credibly suggested that it was Carrie's interference over the accounts and her over-diligent auditorship that precipitated the final row. One may suspect too that it was Carrie who kept Kipling (who was no litigant) up to the ill-judged legal proceedings he instituted against Beattie; he won them, but lost far more than he gained, for the thing became a farce and he was laughed out of America. Hence the retreat to England, a series of unsatisfactory residences and finally Batemans.

One cannot overlook this American interlude, for its effect on Kipling's character and outlook can hardly be over-estimated. The man who returned to become the owner of Batemans was suffering from loneliness and disillusion in no ordinary degree. The migration to America had collapsed in most mortifying circumstances and, as if this upheaval were not sufficient, Kipling had lost, in the course of a visit to New York to prosecute the anti-Beattie campaign, his treasured Josephine; she caught a chill on the voyage and died in New York while her father lay himself at death's door, too ill to know what was happening. The American interlude of 1892–9 (dating it from his marriage to Josephine's death) had indeed been critical in Kipling's life; it shattered him; it is impossible for anyone with a grain of imagination to suppose otherwise. Once more, as in that childhood's transition from India to Southsea, the world had turned – for no apparent reason – and rent him, the smiling face of Fortune had darkened to the most hideous of scowls. Kipling came to Sussex and Burwash a man flying before the blast, broken in health by his own grave illness, broken in confidence by unmerited affliction. The man who was to set up house at Batemans was a man flung high and dry on the beach after shipwreck; he was a man finished with adventure, finished with violence, ripe for settlement and peace. If he clung to that beach on which he had been cast up, made much of it, swore never to leave it, can one wonder?

In that shipwreck much indeed had perished; the stranded mariner was now left to himself, to Carrie his wife, and to his two surviving children – John (who was to die near Loos in 1915) and Elsie. It is impossible from Kipling's writings to discover what were his relations towards his wife; that was a matter in which he very properly preserved his strictest privacy and into which one should not attempt to probe. Yet it is difficult not to accuse Mrs Kipling of contributing to her husband's loneliness and of firing his more disagreeable moods; she stood between him and the world in more senses than one. She preserved him no doubt from the importunate, from the cadger, the climber, the battener, and she managed his affairs much better than he could have managed them himself; not in vain or wholly in jest did Kipling refer to her as the 'works manager' or the 'committee of ways and means'. But her proprietary control was adamant. One of Kipling's oldest friends has admitted that in order to remain his intimate it was constantly necessary to placate his wife; new friends, or would-be friends, were vetted relentlessly. In many ways of course this was to Kipling's advantage; left to himself, he might never have known so many of the right people or grown into the pillar of authority he became. Yet the net effect may have been to incarcerate him more and more closely in that solitary cell which was in one mood his choice, in another his abhorrence. Doubtless he enjoyed his chains but chains in a sense they were.

As to his children, he has told us very little about them either. One can see them of course as Dan and Una in *Pook's Hill*, being well-behaved and pleasantly imbibing instruction (as their father would have imbibed it), from Puck, Parnesius, Dalyngridge, Hal o' the Draft, and others. But from that stage onwards they seem to recede. I cannot think of any young man in Kipling's works who could possibly be John or any girl in her teens or twenties who could be Elsie. This of course was right and proper; the writer who uncovers in print the nakedness of his children is guilty of the converse of the sin of Ham which is more disgusting and unforgivable than the original. Yet one cannot but wonder if his children, when they ceased to be children, dwindled correspondingly in Kipling's life; one would like very much to know how they all got along together at Batemans, what family life there was like, and how far it assuaged the loneliness it in other ways accentuated. Kipling was a devoted and impeccable husband – in refreshing contrast to some of his fellow authors of the 'nineties and the early nineteen-hundreds. He must have been a charming and lovable father; one so successful with children in general could hardly fail with his own. Yet despite it all one cannot rid oneself of the feeling that he was, in the second half of his life, a very lonely man. I wish I could think that he who gave such happiness to so many was happy himself.

There he goes – legging it for the Downs, cap on head, stick in hand, his dark defensive face half turned over his shoulder to make sure we are not pursuing him, that he will be left undisturbed to his mood, whatever it may be. He is a man whose success in his chosen work has been transcendent and phenomenal, he is becoming a leading figure not only in the letters but in the life of England, he has spanned the world and made it his plaything, he is the owner of that fine old mansion down yonder among the trees; he is free, independent, settled, rich, acclaimed, and at his zenith. But is Kipling of Batemans, with all these advantages, as happy as he should be?

Batemans, Sussex

One mile south-west of Burwash. Built of stone in 1634 for a prosperous iron-master, and very little altered since that date. Certain rooms are shown, including Kipling's study, which is preserved exactly as he used it till his death in 1936.

T. E. LAWRENCE

By *Sir Ronald Storrs*

L<small>AWRENCE</small> was of less than medium stature and, though slight, strongly built. His forehead was high, his face upright, and, in proportion to the depth of the head, long. His yellow hair was parted and brushed sideways. He had a straight nose, piercing gentian-blue eyes, a firm and very full mouth, a strong square chin and fine, careful, and accomplished hands. His Sam Browne belt was as often as not buckled loose over his unbuttoned shoulder-strap, or he would forget to put it on at all. Once at least I had to send my servant Ismain running with it after him into the street. Augustus John's first drawing is perfect of his Arab period; Kennington's bronze in the crypt of St Paul's Cathedral gives the plastic and Homeric simplicity of his lines and rhythm; and Howard Coster's photograph, published in *The Illustrated London News* after his death, besides being a good likeness hints somehow at the unhappiness latent behind the eyes. Most revealing perhaps of all is Kennington's 'Ghost Portrait', now hanging in All Souls College, Oxford, and reproduced in *Orientations*.

Save for official purposes he hated fixed times and seasons. I would come upon him in my Cairo flat, reading always Latin or Greek, with corresponding gaps in my shelves. But he put back in their proper places the books he did not take away; of those he took he left a

Cloud's Hill, DORSET

list, and never failed to return them reasonably soon, in perfect condition. We had no literary differences, except that he preferred Homer to Dante and disliked my placing Theocritus before Aristophanes. He loved music, harmony rather than counterpoint, and would sit back against the cushions with his eyes half-closed, enduring even that meander of musical consciousness which I dignified by the name of improvisation. He used to ask at the door if I was alone, and go away if I was not; fearing (he told me when I complained) that he might be let in for the smart 'or' the boring – he meant 'and', for the terms with him were synonymous. He angered me once by failing (without excuse) to appear at a dinner of four I had arranged for him; and only told me afterwards that I had more than 'got back on him' by explaining that I shouldn't have minded if he had only warned me in time to get somebody else.

He was eager and unfatigued in bazaar-walking and mosque-hunting. I found him from the beginning an arresting and an intentionally provocative talker, liking nonsense to be treated as nonsense, and not civilly or dully accepted or dismissed. He could flame into sudden anger at a story of pettiness, particularly official pettiness or injustice.

Shortly after the Arab Revolution we found that its success was denied or blanketed by the enemy press (which was of course quoted by neutrals) and we decided that the best proof that it had taken place would be provided by an issue of Hejaz postage stamps which would carry the Arab propaganda, self-paying and incontrovertible, to the four corners of the earth. The

Foreign Office approved. I wandered with Lawrence round the Arab Museum in Cairo collecting suitable arabesque motifs. It was quickly apparent that Lawrence already possessed or had immediately assimilated a complete working technique of philatelic and three-colour reproduction, so that he was able to supervise the issue from start to finish. And it seemed only a few weeks before this young Hittite archæologist was on the most intimate terms with machine-guns, with tulip bombs, even with the jealously forbidden subtleties of a Roll-Royce engine. There still exists the last motor-cycle built for him; never ridden, never delivered, carrying ten improvements, all invented by himself.

The Amir[1] Abdullah was deeply impressed with his extraordinary detailed knowledge of 'enemy dispositions' which, being temporary Sub-Lieutenant in charge of 'maps and marking of Turkish Army distribution', he was able to use with masterly effect. As Syrian, Circassian, Anatolian, Mesopotamian names came up, Lawrence at once stated exactly which unit was in each position, until Abdullah turned to me in amazement: 'Is this man God, to know everything?'

Early in January 1918 I was sitting in a snowbound Jerusalem, when an orderly announced a Bedouin, and Lawrence walked in and sat beside me. He remained for the rest of the day, and left me temporarily the poorer by a Virgil and a Catullus. Later on, when in Jerusalem, he always stayed in my house, an amusing as well as an absorbing if sometimes disconcerting guest. He had Shelley's trick of noiselessly vanishing and reappearing. We

[1] Now King.

would be sitting reading on my only sofa: I would look up, and Lawrence was not only not in the room, he was not in the house, he was not in Jerusalem. He was in the train on his way to Egypt.

In those days and (owing to the withering hand of Monsieur Mavromatis's Ottoman concession) for years after, there was no electric light in Jerusalem, and in my early bachelor household the hands of the Arab servants fell heavy upon the incandescent mantles of our paraffin lamps, from which a generous volcano of filthy smuts would nightly stream over the books, the carpets, and everything in the room. Lawrence took the lamp situation daily in hand, and so long as he was there all was bright on the Aladdin front. He said he liked the house because it contained the necessities and not the tiresomenesses of life; that is to say there were a few Greek marbles, a good piano, and a great many books, though (I fear) not enough towel-horses, no huckabacks, and a very irregular supply of cruets and dinner-napkins. Not all my guests agreed with Lawrence's theory; but the Egyptian cook did, for my servant Said once observed: 'When your Excellency has none other than "Urenz" in the house, Abd al-Wahhab prepares *ala kaifu* – without bothering himself.'

He was not (any more than Kitchener) a misogynist, though he would have retained his composure if he had been suddenly informed that he would never see a woman again. He could be charming to people like my wife and sister, whom he considered to be 'doing' something, but he regarded (and sometimes treated) with embarrassing horror those who merely 'dressed, and knew people'.

When at a dinner-party, a lady illustrated her anecdotes with the Christian names, nick-names, and pet-names of famous (and always titled) personages, Lawrence's dejection became so obvious that the lady, leaning incredulously forward, asked: 'I fear my conversation does not interest Colonel Lawrence very much?' Lawrence bowed from the hips – and those were the only muscles that moved: 'It does not interest me at all,' he answered.

I was standing with him one morning in the Continental Hotel, Cairo, waiting to start for work in the Arab Bureau, when an elderly Englishwoman, quite incapable of understanding his talk, but anxious to be seen conversing with the Uncrowned King of Arabia, moved towards him. It was hot, and she was fanning herself with a newspaper as she introduced herself: 'Just think, Colonel Lawrence, ninety-two! Ninety-two.' With a tortured smile he replied: 'Many happy returns of the day!'

In those days he spoke much of the press he would found in Epping Forest for the printing of classics, where he said: 'I'll pull you the Theocritus of your dreams. I'm longing to get back to my printing-press, but I have two kings to make first.' He made the kings if not the press: Faisal in Iraq, Abdullah in Transjordan stand indeed as in part his creations.

I asked him once point-blank why he was doing what he was doing – and not more. He answered that there was only one thing in the world worth being, and that was a creative artist. He had tried to be this, and had failed. He said: 'I know I can write a good sentence, a good paragraph, even a good chapter, but I have proved I

116

cannot write a good book.' Not having yet seen *Seven Pillars* I could only quote the praise of David Hogarth (which meant much to Lawrence) and agree that, compared with the glory of *Hamlet* or *The Divine Comedy*, career was nothing. Still, admitting these to be unattainable, there were Prime Ministers, Archbishops, Admirals of the Fleet, press barons, and philanthropic millionaires, some of whom rendered service surely preferable to this utter renunciation? He allowed the principle, but refused the application. Since he could not be what he would, he would be nothing: the minimum existence, work without thought; and when he left the Royal Air Force it would be as night-watchman in a City warehouse.

For all his puckishness, his love of disconcerting paradox, I believed then and am certain now that Lawrence meant what he said; though I thought there was also the element of dismay at the standard expected of him by the public; and I doubted how far even his nerves could ever be the same after his hideous man-handling in Deraa.

I further believe that, though not given to self-depreciation, he did underrate the superlative excellence of *Seven Pillars*, and, as a most conscious artist in words, ached to go farther still. He loved discussing his own prose and, if convinced, was humble under criticism, whether of style or of fact. Thus he did not dissent when I thought that his *Odyssey* sacrificed overmuch to the desire of differing from predecessors, for instance, in rendering ῥοδοδάκτυλος ἠώς – rosy-fingered dawn – in nineteen different ways. It is therefore an arresting rather than a satisfying version. Lawrence, though respectful almost to deference of expert living authority, lacked the surrender of soul to submit himself lowly and reverently, even to the first of poets. Of Matthew Arnold's three requisites for translating Homer – simplicity, speed, and nobility, all dominating qualities of Lawrence's being – he failed somehow in presenting the third, substituting as often as not some defiant and most un-Homeric puckishness of his own, so that Dr Bentley's criticism of Pope's *Iliad*—a very pretty poem, Mr Pope, but not Homer—would be no less applicable to Lawrence's Revised Version of the *Odyssey*. The classical Arab could become in a trice a street Arab. Nevertheless, Lawrence's *Odyssey* possesses two outstanding merits. It represents Lawrence as well as Homer, and it has by hero-worship or the silken thread of snobbishness drawn to Homer thousands that could never have faced the original, or even the renderings of Pope, Chapman, or Butcher and Lang.

He hated public attention save when impersonal enough for him to appear not to notice it, but was not disappointed when, as nearly always, his incognito broke down. One day he offered to take my wife and me to the Imperial War Museum 'to see the Orpens'. When we came to his portrait by James McBey, I asked him to stand in front so that we might for a minute see him against McBey's vision. In a flash the word went round the staff that Lawrence was here, and for the rest of our visit we were accompanied by the rhythmic beat of a dozen martial heels. Lawrence was clearly not displeased, yet when on our departure I remarked upon the number of our escort, 'Really?' he said. 'I didn't notice any one.' He was indeed a mass of contradictions: shy and retiring, yet he positively enjoyed sitting for and criticizing his portrait. No one could have been more remote from the standard of the public school, and I can as easily picture him in a frock-coat or in hunting pink as in an old school tie. In action likewise he was an individual force of driving intelligence, but with nothing of the administrator, having about as much team spirit as Alexander the Great or Mr Lloyd George.

In England we met (as might have been expected) more often unexpectedly than by appointment – in the street, on a bus, or at a railway station. Once, when I was choosing gramophone records, a hand from behind descended firmly upon my shoulder. I had only just arrived in England, and supposed for a moment that this must be an attempt on the part of an assistant at Brighter British Salesmanship. It was Lawrence, replenishing the immense collection of records arranged in volumes round a square of deep shelves in the upper room of his cottage. On another occasion he led me to his publishers where, walking round the room, he picked out half a dozen expensive books, and, as though he were the head of the firm, made me a present of them. He was a loyal, unchanging, and affectionate friend, and would charge down from London on the iron steed, from which he met his death, to visit me in a nursing home, or run up 200 miles from the West of England to say good-bye before I returned to Cyprus.

Lawrence hated Society, but loved company. He refused the post of Director of Archæology in Cyprus because of what he chose to imagine the social obligations of an official there. Those who knew him could have predicted the comparative failure of his Fellowship of All Souls, where it is reasonably expected of members to mingle with their fellows and, if not indeed to roll the ghost of an Olympian (a Cambridge accomplishment), at least to present to the Common Room on occasion a polished spook of Horace. 'Conversation,' said Gibbon, of the most famous Arab, 'enriches and enlivens the mind, but solitude is the school of genius.'

Nevertheless, Lawrence liked sometimes to walk and talk with friends. The simplicity of his life was extreme. He smoked no tobacco, he drank no alcohol; but alas, he used a drug. His drug was speed, and speed was the dope which cost him his life. He once raced along the open road against an aeroplane, and led it for nearly a quarter of an hour.

Consider the variety of elements in his composition. It has been given to few to achieve greatness and also to enshrine that greatness in splendid prose; to which other of these few has been added the fastidious artistry to plan every detail of the setting up, the illustration, the printing, and the binding of the material presentation of his genius? On any topic he was one of those who let fall, whether in speech or writing, the creative and illuminating idea or phrase – unmistakably his, signed all over – which held your memory and recharged your intellectual and spiritual batteries.

The secret of his ascendancy – physical, intellectual, and moral – is best explained in his own words: 'Among the Arabs there were no distinctions, traditional or natural, except the unconscious power given a famous shaikh by virtue of his accomplishment; and they taught me that no man could be their leader except he ate the rank's food, wore their clothes, lived level with them, and yet appeared better in himself.'

He could be the best company in the world, holding his own with Winston Churchill or Bernard Shaw: he could also retire within himself, with paralysing effect upon any company. He preferred the society of men to that of women, with very few exceptions. He was a fine judge of painting and sculpture and had a true appreciation of music, which he trained (and gratified) on a large collection of carefully tended gramophone records.

Into his style, based originally upon that of his venerated Doughty's *Arabia Deserta*, Lawrence poured the conscious, conscientious devotion of the artist-craftsman which he had lavished upon his maps, his machinery, and his plans for battle. 'Words,' he wrote, 'get richer every time they are deliberately used ... but only when deliberately used', and again, more significantly, 'Writing has been my inmost self all my life, and I can never put my full strength into anything else.'

Some knew one side of Lawrence, some another. I wondered then if any knew him at all, or could imagine what had been his purpose, what the frontiers of his being. Could he have grown old? Had he ever been young? Some think he intended to resume action for his country. Others that he would have created at least one more great work, for like Plato he felt deeply that what gives life its value is the sight, however revealed, of Eternal Beauty. In this he is with the great Elizabethans – Sir Philip Sidney; with the great Victorians – Charles

Gordon – whose whole lives, free from fear and gain (those old perverters of mankind), are a protest against the guaranteed, the pensioned, the standardized, and the safety-first existence.

None can begin to realize the unsuspected, the bewildering variety and versatility of Lawrence, before as well as after his Arabian exploits, until they have read his Letters, selected and edited by David Garnett in 1938. It has been said that he would have survived, as would Edward Fitzgerald even without Omar Khayyám, if only as a letter-writer. But even these utterly fail to explain the strange blend of contrasts and oppositions that made up his elusive, enigmatic, and paradoxical personality. Imperious but retiring, logical yet intuitive, profoundly impressive and impishly puckish, on equal terms with Field Marshals and Cabinet Ministers, great writers, mechanics, scholars, and slaves, he has bequeathed to youth in general – and not least to British youth – the example of one who combined physical prowess and courage under the open sky with passionate self-dedication to the testament of the great humanities; and so remains, even without his work, without his book, a standard and a touchstone of reality in life.

Cloud's Hill, Dorset

Nine miles east of Dorchester, just north of Bovington Camp on the Wool–Puddletown road. A small brick-and-tile cottage; the interior, with its austere furnishings, remains virtually unaltered since Lawrence's death. Open to the public at certain times.

Flint Cottage, BOX HILL, SURREY

GEORGE MEREDITH

By Walter Allen

As much as his own Sir Willoughby Patterne, whose presence and splendour the adoring Mrs Mountstuart summed up in the single piercing phrase, 'You see he has a leg', George Meredith was born to impress. Even at the age of ten, the neighbouring small boys – playmates one can scarcely call them; one of them remembered fifty years after how Meredith would pass by with a drawled 'How de do, Price' – knew him as 'gentleman Georgy', and the epithet seems not at all to have been a gibe, but the simple recognition of evident superiority. This cloak of superiority he carried with him throughout his life. Partly, it was an attribute of his physical beauty, which struck all who met him. When he was thirty or so, Rossetti used him as the model for the head of Christ in his painting 'Mary Magdalene at the Gate of Simon the Pharisee'; while in his extreme old age, according to Mr Desmond MacCarthy, who visited him several times at Flint Cottage, 'his face beneath a tousled thatch of hair, soft as the finest wood-ash, and combed down into a fringe upon a high round forehead, had a noble, ravaged handsomeness', even though the 'keen look in profile, as of an upward-pointing arrow, had gone'. This beauty of brow and countenance was not in the least epicene or fragile. His novels and poetry would be enough to show that he, if ever there was one, was a man of the open air. But he was more than this. He was a man who rejoiced in violent physical exertion, who boxed, fenced, exercised daily with what he called the 'beetle' – a mallet weighing eighteen or nineteen pounds which he would throw in the air and catch by the handle – and indulged in those feats of pedestrianism which seem now to have been almost the occupational neurosis of Victorian men of letters. He rejoiced, too, in wine and food – his first published book was a cookery book, written in collaboration with his first wife. And if men appreciated him, so did women, and he them. As we glimpse him in middle life, through the memoirs of his friends, he appears little less than a force of nature, a titan roaring with laughter and song and shouting his epigrams in the teeth of the wind.

He was born to impress, both by his presence and by his art, and impress he did, until at the turn of the century, as Mr E. M. Forster has said, at his name 'much of the universe and all Cambridge trembled'; and this though he maintained until the end of his life, and in the face of all the evidence, that no one read him and that the critics ignored him. Yet even while he impressed – perhaps it was one reason why he impressed – he remained enigmatic. It has often been observed that his novels, compared with those of contemporaries from Dickens to Hardy and beyond, are curiously lacking in background, that they seldom give the feeling of a definite place at a definite date. And Meredith himself strangely lacked a background. There the man in all his splendour, brilliance, and poetry; he could no more be avoided than the south-west wind he loved; and yet – who was he?

and where did he come from? No use, even if one had dared, asking him: he was the most reticent, the most secretive of men. Thus, one of his closest friends, William Hardman, later editor of the *Morning Post*, did not know that his first wife, from whom he had parted in much the way described in *Modern Love*, was the daughter of the novelist Thomas Love Peacock, until he read the dedication in Meredith's first and, to all intents and purposes, suppressed book of verse in the British Museum. And the obvious works of reference yielded remarkably little; nothing beyond the date of his birth, 12th February, 1828, and a vague birthplace, Hampshire. Given the man, with his personality and genius, it was impossible not to speculate upon his origins. And those who speculated, even though they were not to know it, were taking part in something that, if it happened in fiction, we should certainly have to call a typical Meredithian comedy.

If the speculations appear fantastic to us it is, partly at any rate, because we are not under the personal spell of the man. He must be, it was agreed, illegitimate, and since he was illegitimate he could not be less than of noble birth, though the details of his paternity could be disputed. One school of thought, determined that the paternity should be as illustrious as possible, claimed that he was the natural son of George IV; another that his father was William IV; a third, perhaps because no obvious trace could be found in his manner and appearance, to say nothing of his talent, of anything characteristically Hanoverian, was content to believe that Bulwer-Lytton was his father. Yet the truth was in its way scarcely less fantastic than the conjectures, for Meredith had already made public the facts and origins of his family in his novel *Evan Harrington*, made them so public, indeed, that in some instances he had not even bothered to change the names of characters he had taken directly from life.

Like Evan Harrington himself, Meredith had been born the son of a tailor of Portsmouth. That was his secret; and because he never divulged it he has, naturally enough, been accused of being a snob. The charge is altogether too superficial. It is beside the point to say that the tailor's is an honourable trade and that by Meredith's time the family was distinguished enough – one of his aunts was the wife of a general of Marines who had been knighted for his services, and the daughter of another was married to the Portuguese nobleman who was ambassador to the Vatican. Meredith's maladjustment went far deeper than simple snobbery. His pride was such that fully to express it one would need to fall back on the Latin word *superbia*, with its connotations on the one hand of arrogance and superciliousness, on the other of grandeur and high-mindedness. It was a pride, one guesses, that made him utterly incapable of admitting that he could be inferior to anyone or ever less than right. It is possible that he saw himself as a sort of changeling, that he was possessed by that common dream of children who, loving their parents, yet feel that if justice were done their heritage would be vastly different, believe, though rationally they know it to be nonsense, that they are stolen princesses, heirs to thrones of which they have been robbed. If it were so, then Meredith belonged to the third generation of a family of such changelings. Dominating *Evan Harrington*, for all that he is dead before the action proper begins, is the figure of the 'Great Mel', the gentleman-tailor who shook hands as an equal with his customers and never sent out a bill, who rode to hounds and was an officer in the Yeomanry Cavalry, who was taken for a marquis when visiting Bath, who was laughed at by the gentry for his grand, untailor-like behaviour, and yet was respected and even admired by them for the way in which he carried it off without ever pretending to be other than what he was. The 'Great Mel' was a portrait of Melchizedek Meredith, 'Gentleman Georgy's' grandfather. As might be expected, he died and left only his debts and his shop to his family. To pay off the debts so that his memory should not be dishonoured, his son, however unwillingly, had to forgo his own ambitions toward the status of gentleman, abandon his career as a medical student, and become a tailor in his turn; this at the behest of his mother, the simple, dignified woman who is as much the true heroine of *Evan Harrington* as her husband is its true hero.

Bearing his heredity in mind, we can realize the strain imposed on George Meredith from his earliest days. He bore it heroically, and the persona – compounded not only of pride, which was sometimes unpleasant enough, as his behaviour to his father and to his first wife shows, but also of the inflexible sense of honour which came perhaps from his grandmother – with which he faced the world never seems to have cracked. It is true that we know the day-to-day details of his life far less intimately than we do those of Dickens and Thackeray, for instance, but signs of uneasiness behind the mask are few. When they occur, they do so in the way we should expect, in manifestations of arrogance and ostentation; his close friend Mrs Ross, who had been the model as a girl both for Rose Jocelyn in *Evan Harrington* and for Clara Middleton in *The Egoist*, noted that 'before strangers his shyness took the form of asserting himself too loudly, and trying to be epigrammatic and witty; he gave one the impression that he was not quite sure on what footing he stood'. Yet it seems to me that it is in his prose, his too consciously epigrammatic, rococo style, that the underlying sense of strain, of maladjustment, is most clearly seen.

To some writers, Meredith has seemed an adventurer; and we have only to look at the character of Richmond Roy in *The Adventures of Harry Richmond* and the gusto that informs that wonderful creation to realize that if his ambitions had been other than literary he might truly have been one. Other critics, observing the contradiction between the behaviour of the man himself and the theme and purpose of his fiction, have regretted that he was less than his books. But it is doubtful if any author is as great as his work, doubtful indeed if it is possible; and though the contradiction is not to be denied, it plainly lies near the heart of his creativeness as a novelist.

For what is the overriding theme and purpose of his fiction? It can be summed up in the words in which he describes the function of the Comic Spirit in his great *Essay on the Idea of Comedy*: —

'Men's future on earth does not attract it; their honesty and shapeliness in the present does; and whenever they wax out of proportion, overblown, affected, pretentious, bombastical, hypocritical, pedantic, fantastically delicate; whenever it sees them self-deceived or hoodwinked, given to run riot on idolatries, drifting into vagaries, congregating in absurdities, planning short-sightedly, plotting dementedly; whenever they are at variance with their professions, and violate the unwritten but perceptible laws binding them in consideration one to another; whenever they offend sound reason, fair justice; are false in humility or mined with conceit, individually, or in the bulk – the Spirit overhead will look humanely malign and cast an oblique light on them, followed by volleys of silvery laughter.'

It is in the oblique light of the Comic Spirit that Meredith scrutinizes and exposes the excesses of the personality, whether they reveal themselves as sentimentalism, egoism, overweening pride, or the sense of superiority which makes the individual think himself wiser than his fellows and the traditions of his time. R. L. Stevenson reports that a young man once expostulated angrily with Meredith, after the publication of *The Egoist*: 'It's too bad of you, Willoughby is me!' To which Meredith retorted: 'My dear fellow, he is all of us.' Certainly the egoist Sir Willoughby was Meredith; and matching his work against his life, we can now see that when writing his satirical fiction, Meredith, as much as any writer who ever lived, was following the command of Sir Philip Sidney's muse, 'Look in thy heart, and write'. In a very real sense, he was satirizing himself; all his great comic creations represent recognizable aspects of Meredith, and it is significant that the characters who stand for common sense, right values, and right behaviour are pale shadows by comparison.

But Meredith was a poet as well as a satirist, and he was never more a poet than in his fiction. Poetry adds a dimension to his work not often found in intellectual comedy. And his is an ardent poetry, springing out of a delighted appreciation of the beauty of nature and the beauty and vitality of women. It flashes out in his novels not only in magical phrases and images but also in sustained lyrical passages, such as the marvellous description of first love, in *The Ordeal of Richard Feverel*, or the picture of Clara Middleton standing against the wild cherry tree in bloom, in *The Egoist*. It is this transcending quality of his poetry that makes Stevenson's description, in a letter to Henley, still the best account we have of the nature of Meredith's fiction: 'Beauty, touched with sex and laughter; beauty with God's earth for the background. ... Comedy which keeps the beauty and touches the terrors of our life (laughter and tragedy-in-a-good-humour having kissed) ...; embracing the greatest number of elements of fate and character; and telling its story, not with the one eye of pity, but with the two of pity and mirth.'

Meredith's poetry has worn less well than his fiction, though it would be absurd to deny that the writer of *Modern Love*, *Love in a Valley*, *The Lark Ascending*, and the superb sonnet *Lucifer in Starlight*, among other works, was less than a great poet. But beneath much of his verse one feels, for all its brilliance, a hard core of prose. It is not so much that his poetry is difficult as that it is difficult in the wrong way. The meaning can be disengaged with a little patience, but too often it has not been fused with the metaphors – the over-proliferation of metaphors – in which it is expressed. One feels that one is being got at, that the passion behind the poetry is rhetorical rather than purely poetic, and that one is being got at in the name of a philosophy which will not stand close examination. Meredith was a worshipper of nature, more precisely, of the earth: –

> Earth, the mother of all,
> Moves on her stedfast way,
> Gathering, flinging, sowing.
> Mortals, we live in her day,
> She in her children growing.

And earth, he believed, if accepted with courage, with affirmation, would console as well as delight; to quote two of his finest and most famous lines: –

> Into the breast that gives the rose,
> Shall I with shuddering fall?

He has been seen, therefore, as the poet of the idea of Evolution. Yet the fact is, if his philosophy is to have universal validity, the landscape of Surrey, which so often inspires its poetic expression, charming as it is, is not adequate to carry it. It is difficult to resist Mr E.M. Forster's taunt: 'The home counties posing as the universe.' The woods near Abinger, for instance, which partly suggested *The Woods of Westermain* ('Enter these enchanted woods, You who dare'), cannot with propriety symbolize the nature which includes the swamps and forests of the Amazon and the aridities of the Arabian Desert. To enter those an altogether different kind of daring is required.

Meredith's philosophy, then, was too localized to its time and place to endure. He was not a widely travelled man, but the scenes he knew he loved: Italy, the Alps, the Rhineland, which he had learnt as a boy at school at Neuwied, above all, the pastoral southern English countryside of Hampshire and Surrey, which is the main background of his novels. It is unlikely that the novels will ever recover the popularity which they lost with his death in 1909. He had dominated his age for so long that a reaction against them was inevitable; and in any case his death more or less coincided with the rise of a much more direct style of writing than he was willing to give anywhere except in *Modern Love*, that subtle analysis in memorable and often great poetry of incompatibility of temperament leading to tragedy which is probably his most widely read work today. The grand manner – and Meredith's was a version of the grand manner – became of itself suspect, and we have still to lose our distrust of the magnificently self-confident generalizations in which he commented on life and which seemed so profound to the intelligent young of his age. All the same, it is not easy to account fully for the neglect into which his novels have largely fallen, for, when criticism has said its worst against them, the best of them remain remarkable works. Certainly they contain some of the finest characters in our fiction, characters that are a constant delight: The 'Great Mel', Mrs Harrington and the Countess in *Evan Harrington*; the 'wise youth' Adrian in *The Ordeal of Richard Feverel*; Richmond Roy and Squire Beltham in *The Adventures of Harry Richmond*; Nevil Beauchamp in *Beauchamp's Career*; Sir Willoughby Patterne in *The*

Egoist; besides a group of young women whose match it would be hard to find outside Shakespeare and Jane Austen, women who possess beauty, wit, character, and charm in equal proportions and who are always vivid to the reader's senses. And all are exposed in the urbane light of his comedy, while the women are transfigured also by the radiance of his poetry.

It is in his novels that we find the essential Meredith. The man fascinates but is scarcely lovable; we who never came under his personal spell will probably find his pride repellent. But we have only to read the novels and glance at the portraits of him to understand the potency of the spell, to understand why year after year the brightest spirits among his younger contemporaries made the pilgrimage to Flint Cottage, where, never rich, he lived like a nobleman incognito for more than forty years, regaling them with the wines he wrote about so well, dazzling them with his loud, flashing, epigram-studded conversation which was made up, as his greatest admirer Stevenson tells us, of 'veracity ... and high athletic intellectual humbug', and warming them with his unquenchable vitality.

Flint Cottage, Surrey

About 250 yards north of the Burford Bridge Hotel at Box Hill. An early nineteenth-century cottage of brick with flint facings and a slate roof. There is no admittance.

ISAAC NEWTON

By Professor H. Levy

THE seventeenth century stands in bold characters as the epoch in which the mysticism of the Middle Ages and the dogmas of the ancients melted like snow in the new climate of knowledge and of its rational analysis. As the geographical barriers between peoples were swept aside by the rising tide of trade between East and West, commodity exchange increased, and the arts and crafts expanded to meet this hastening need. Merchant ships broke into hitherto uncharted oceans, and the theory and instrumentation of navigation were called urgently to help in the accurate determination of position at sea. To their aid came the newly invented telescope that threw a flood of light on the heavenly bodies, and enabled the sky to be mapped out with detailed accuracy. In this way the fundamental data for a new science of astronomy were massing, ready to reveal the secrets of planetary order, once a mind was born with sufficient skill to carry through the tremendous task of analysis.

Society in its own way prepared the ground. For the new knowledge that now poured in, and the consequent mood of rapid change that stirred Europe, meant a highly charged atmosphere that set the imagination aflame, and drove minds prospecting in utterly new directions. A generation was coming to life with a new boldness of

Woolsthorpe Manor, WOOLSTHORPE, LINCOLNSHIRE

thought. The sky, always largely a source of mystical wonder, began to rearrange itself and the movement of its parts into something approaching system and order. If the spirit of this epoch must be expressed in terms of individuals, then the names that stand out in this historic effort to unravel the web of nature are those of Copernicus, Galileo, Kepler, and Newton.

On the grand planetary scale Copernicus drew in bold strokes what Darwin later sketched in meticulous detail for the animal world. He unseated man from his egocentric position in the heavens, and deposited him on one of the minor planets revolving round the sun. Copernicus' picture was descriptive, qualitative. It is to Galileo that the credit must be given for showing that, if in the last resort an appeal is made by direct measurable experiment to nature itself instead of to accepted tradition, natural law will show itself in a regular and systematic way. Processes could be made to repeat. Kepler, perhaps more of a mystic than a scientist, by a remarkable *tour de force* of arithmetic, analysed a vast mass of accumulated astronomical data and showed that the apparently complex motions of the planets, regarded as revolving in Copernican fashion round the sun, could be resolved into three simple regularities of behaviour: –

1. The planets revolved in ellipses around the sun with the latter at a point known as the focus.

2. A line joining the sun to any moving planet swept out equal areas in equal times. This meant that the planets were a type of astronomical clock moving with unfailing regularity.

3. For all the planets, irrespective of the length of their

year, i.e. the time taken to make a complete circuit of the sun, and irrespective of their distances from the sun, the square of the length of their year divided by the cube of their distances was always the same number.

This resolution of outwardly chaotic measurements into law and order was a tremendous achievement, because, be it noted, Kepler had not set up his own experiment nor designed the circumstances to bring out this regularity. He had, perforce, to take and to analyse nature's own experiment, the motion of the planetary system as he found it, and to dig out these regularities from the hidden depths.

To him these were three quite independent laws, in no way linked together by any general underlying theory. In a sense they were simply a clear way of assembling his arithmetical data. Yet the dim perception of a rationale of nature was still enmeshed in a tangle of mysticism. To Kepler the planets were urged on their courses by the power of angels. He sought no natural explanation.

Into this semi-emancipated mental atmosphere Newton was born in the year Galileo died. If mathematical and analytical capacity are at all inherited, Newton must have drawn his qualities in this respect from his father's rather than his mother's side. The former, a rather wild and erratic young man, died before Newton was born. His mother married again, but none of Newton's half-sisters or half-brothers gave any signs of the genius that gripped Isaac. As a youngster, disinclined to sport, he showed a remarkable ingenuity in the constructing of many mechanical toys, kites, windmills, and even when quite young constructed a wooden clock that worked, a remarkable achievement in those days. Part of a sun-dial he made is still preserved at the Royal Society. It was, however, his maternal uncle who sensed something of the capacity that was latent in the boy. It was he who finally succeeded in obtaining his entry into Trinity College, Cambridge, in 1660, where he paid his way partly by performing menial tasks in the college. Here Newton found himself under the inspiring influence of Barrow, the first Lucasian Professor of Geometry. This was the year of the Restoration, troublous years when blind Milton was in hiding for his anti-Royalist views, the year of the founding of the Royal Society. Seven years later the master stood down to make way for his successor – his brilliant pupil Isaac Newton.

The years 1665–6 saw the Great Plague sweep across England; and Newton returned to the seclusion of Woolsthorpe to escape its danger. This rest from the immediate drive of studies and lectures was precisely what Newton needed at this time – the opportunity to turn, undisturbed by college activities, to the sorting and sifting of the problems which, as he had already perceived, had to be overcome before the next phase of scientific advance could be entered. During these two years, perhaps the most fertile two years in the history of man's creative work, Newton made advances in mathematics and mathematical physics that would have done credit to a whole generation of busy scientists of normal stature. By the time he had returned to Cambridge he had practically laid the foundations for the scientific work that was to engage the attention of mathematicians, mathematical physicists, and engineers for a century or more –

the three Laws of Motion of material bodies, the Theory of Gravitation, the Theory of the Tides, the Figure of the Earth, the Composition of Light, and, on the mathematical side, the Calculus. This was the astonishing performance of a young man in his twenties; and although it is true that much of it was worked out by him in detail in later years, it is clear enough that the broad outline of his programme and the plan of his attack were already sharply conceived before he returned to his college activities.

In a manuscript found among the Portsmouth papers Newton gives an amazing picture of the activity of his mind at this time: –

'In the beginning of the year 1665 I found the method of approximating series, and the rule for reducing any dignity of any binomial into such a series.[1] The same year in May I found the method of tangents of Gregory and Slusius, and in November had the direct method of fluxions,[2] and the next year in January had the theory of colours, and in May following I had entrance into the inverse method of fluxions.[3] And the same year I began to think of gravity extending to the orb of the Moon, and having found out how to estimate the force with which a globe revolving within a sphere presses the surface of the sphere, from Kepler's rule of the periodical times of the planets being in a sesquialternate proportion of their distances from the centres of their orbs, I deduced that the forces which keep the planets in their orbs must be reciprocally as the squares of their distances from the

---

[1] The Binomial Theorem.   [2] The Differential Calculus.
[3] The Integral Calculus.

centres about which they revolve: and thereby compared the force requisite to keep the Moon in her orb with the force of gravity at the surface of the earth, and found them answer pretty nearly. All this was in the two plague years of 1665 and 1666, for in those days I was in the prime of my age for invention, and minded Mathematicks and Philosophy more than at any time since.'

An individual has to cope with the problems of his age, and attempt to resolve them with the tools his society has forged. Genius shows itself in an acute power to select the significant elements in these problems, to burrow down to their very core and essence, and, if necessary, to forge new intellectual tools specially designed to resolve them. While others might blunder along, reaching their objective by trial and error, Newton moved directly towards his goal. To grasp the crude magnitude and the architectural grandeur of Newton's achievement we have to appreciate something of the problems his generation had posed. The men who preceded Newton had shown clearly that a wealth of regularity existed in nature, provided it could be disentangled from a multitude of apparently unregulated happenings, but how to disentangle it, and whether the wide variety of regularity reflected some deeper underlying principles, were by no means so obvious. If, for example, the three laws of Kepler could be knit together into one more basic law, from which the three could be deduced, it was not unlikely that this itself would provide the key to a much wider understanding, and suggest new forms of regularity hitherto unsuspected. Newton in fact set himself the task of doing for Cosmology, and for the motion of bodies generally, what the Greeks had done for Geometry, viz. to construct a logical system with the minimum number of hypotheses from which the characteristic changes in nature could be deduced; to create a system of logical determinism that would reflect the causal determinism already seen to exist in certain aspects of nature. The stupendous magnitude of this undertaking might well have appalled a whole generation of mathematicians, but basically Newton's genius lay in the fact that he realized precisely the nature of the task he proposed. Others before him, notably Descartes, had speculated on the possibility. The formulation of the problem was one thing; the nature of the hypotheses from which he must commence and the kind of symbolical tools of a logical or mathematical nature adapted to this end were quite other matters. Newton formulated his problem, set out his fundamental laws which were in fact his hypotheses (although he repudiated hypotheses as such, maintaining that his assumptions were simply established fact), and devised the necessary logical tools. The rest followed because he possessed the technique to apply them. Succeeding generations of mathematicians may have unveiled many hidden assumptions in his work of which Newton was unconscious in his time, they may have cast doubts on the rigour of his logic and on the generality of his results – all this is indeed true, but this would be a false basis on which to estimate the quality of his work. A man must be measured by the yardstick of his day, and on that scale Newton was a giant. Einstein could not have existed in

Newton's time. Two hundred and fifty years of human experience had to be won before the scientific world was ready for the next turn of the screw, and that turn was possible mainly because of the power that Newton had originally exerted.

When set out in isolated terms, Newton's architectural scheme, as becomes an artistic effort, was simplicity itself. His Three Laws of Motion stated – first, what happened to a body in isolation in free space, viz. that it possessed inertia and continued in a state of regular motion in a straight line; secondly, what effect was produced on the motion of a body when pressed forward by a force, viz. that it was accelerated by an amount proportional to that force; thirdly, what was the inter-active effect of two bodies in motion when they impacted on each other, viz. that in such a situation the total amount of momentum in the whole system remained unchanged. We need not here examine these laws in greater detail. It suffices merely to point out that, assuming their validity, an examination of the forces at work in any situation would enable the consequent changes in the motion of the parts to be traced out.

Thereafter what remained was to discover the forces at work in nature, and this was the task of the experimentalist. The fact that a body, when suspended by a spring from a fixed point, stretched that spring was already accepted as evidence that the body was drawn towards the Earth by a force, viz. its weight. The fact that for the same body and spring the stretch was less the further the body was from sea level showed that the force of attraction diminished with the distance between body and Earth. Newton for his purpose made an induction – a generalization – that *every* particle in the Universe attracted every other particle with a force that increased with the masses of the attracting bodies but fell off with the square of the distance between them. This was his famous Law of Gravitation – usually associated with the story of the apple that fell to Earth. Actually, he saw its necessity if Kepler's first rule about elliptical motion of the planets was to be fulfilled.

For a study of the motion of a planet round the Sun what was required now therefore was a direct application of his laws of motion, combined with this statement of the Law of Gravitation. If the Sun be imagined fixed in position, and the Earth be thrown off sideways from a point some distance from the Sun, then the problem of determining the path or orbit traced out by the planet was reduced to a direct one of mathematical calculation. Provided the mathematical technique was to hand the problem was solved in principle. As we have indicated, Newton devised the correct mathematical technique, solved the problem, and showed that in such circumstances the planet would rotate round the Sun along an ellipse with the sun at the focus. This was the first of Kepler's Laws. The remaining two followed immediately. Thus the three laws hitherto regarded as quite independent were *deduced* as logical consequences of the general assumptions regarding motion, gravitational force, and the effects of force on change in motion. Newton had demonstrated that it was possible to do with the Mechanics of Matter what the Greeks had done with the Geometry of Space, viz. reduce its study to a logical deductive system. At one stroke Newton had emulated Euclid.

With this to his credit Newton turned to the study of the tides and quickly showed that their rise and fall at various parts of the Earth's surface, and the distinction between spring and neap tides, could be traced in detail to the effects of the attractive forces exerted on the sheet of water which is the ocean, by the Sun and the Moon, as the Earth spun on its axis. To achieve this, to create an analytical method for the study of natural phenomena at this epoch, would in itself have satisfied the life ambition of any one man even had the mathematical tools been available. They were not, and Newton had to turn to the tremendous task of creating them. What this signified should now be clear.

If Newton proposed to apply the deductive methods of the Greeks to the examination of physical processes he had perforce to break down one of the great barriers that had obstructed the advance of Greek thought. To them motion was always something of a puzzle. How could an object 'located' successively at a series of separate points actually be in motion? How could it be at a position and away from it simultaneously? The crux of their difficulty lay, curiously enough, in their concept of number and therefore in their ideas of time and space measurement. Each number was sharply distinguished from every other, no matter how close any two might be to equality. They had no decimal system that makes it easy for the modern man to conceive of a 'continuum' of numbers. Their number system did not allow of the possibility of continuous change from one number to another. Everything proceeded by jumps. By the time of Newton, this arithmetical difficulty had been largely overcome, although it was not until many years later that it was really established on a firm foundation. For him therefore this psychological obstacle did not exist, and he had merely to ask himself the technical question: how, from a knowledge of the changing position of a body, could its speed and acceleration be calculated? Conversely: how, from a knowledge of the acceleration over a range of time, could the speed and position of the body be determined, assuming that these changes occurred continuously? These in simplified form are the two major problems of the differential and integral calculus, and it is obvious, from the way in which Newton stated the relations between forces and accelerations, that unless they could be resolved it would be impossible to handle the problems he had posed for solution.

It is undoubtedly a matter of historical fact that Newton discovered the calculus long before he actually made known to his contemporaries that he had done so. Indeed it was only when other claimants came forward that he disclosed the secrets he had kept so guardedly to himself. The motive behind this secrecy is not yet clearly understood, and one can only speculate from what is known generally about his character. He was admittedly jealous lest the credit for his discoveries should fall to others, as is apparent from the arguments into which he entered on matters of precedence. These were equally concerned with great as with trivial discoveries. His controversies with Hooke on the Law of Gravitation and with Leibnitz on the calculus, in particular, show him in rather a bad light. There was already so much to his mathematical credit, that generosity, one might have expected, would have been easy for him. Instead he fought Hooke fiercely for credit for the formulation of the Gravitation Law, and practically suggested that the idea of the calculus had been filched from him; whereas anyone can see that the system of notation used by Leibnitz was fundamentally different from that used by Newton, and indeed much more fertile for further development. Moreover, looking back on it now with more sophisticated eyes, we find it obvious enough that both problems were 'in the air'; they were crucial for the time, and their clarification could not have been long delayed. If Newton had not done this, others undoubtedly would have, in time. In fact, Newton's teacher Barrow, his predecessor in the Lucasian Chair at Cambridge, had already made considerable contributions to its solution, and it is not easy to disentangle how much Newton owed in this respect to his master. Be that as it may, recognizing even that what is now accepted as the technique of the calculus is more closely akin to the Leibnitz approach than to the Newtonian, the fact remains that it was undoubtedly a corner-stone in mathematical progress.

Why Newton was so averse to communicating his discoveries to others has never been satisfactorily explained, especially when we bear in mind his anxiety that he should receive due recognition. If he really imagined that a discovery like the calculus could for long be shut off from others, it argues not only a profound disdain for his fellow mathematicians, but a lack of appreciation of the inevitability of certain mathematical developments. The explanation may possibly lie in this, a pure conjecture, that he used the calculus to carry through his dynamical investigations, to arrive at the propositions, and then, before presenting them to his contemporaries, rewrote them in a form that suggested they had been found by other means altogether. It is certainly known that it required all the persuasive powers of young Edmund Halley, the astronomer, to induce Newton to begin writing his masterpiece *The Principia* in 1684. There were of course probably financial difficulties in the way, for the cost of publication was largely defrayed by Halley himself. The book, as we have already indicated, reads like a series of Euclidean propositions. Within two years after it was begun, and after its publication had sent a thrill of excitement throughout the scientific world, Newton was elected to the Presidency of the Royal Society, a position he held for twenty-four years. At the age of forty-five he had really completed his life's work. He laid down his pen without a qualm, became Warden and then Master of the Mint, and representative of the University of Cambridge in Parliament. By this time, however, his mind had begun to cloud. He who had done so much to rationalize our outlook on the Universe, to replace 'inspired prophecy' by scientific prediction, turned his energies to a close study of Biblical prophecy as found in the Book of Daniel. His health failed yet he lived on, without any sign of the return of his early mental vigour. His great achievements in the world of mathematical science had come, as it were, almost in a flash, concentrated into a short segment of his long life. It was as if the very intensity of his thinking during these early twenties had exhausted him, and in a few years had worked him out.

He died at the age of eighty-five, and was buried with high honour, in Westminster Abbey. He had brought to consummation the arduous labours of his predecessors, had torn the veil of mysticism from the face of nature, and completed the theory that was to lighten the way towards the new era of the machine, and all it was to mean for social change.

Woolsthorpe Manor, Lincolnshire

Seven miles south of Grantham, in the village of Woolsthorpe, close to Colsterworth, which is just off the west side of the Great North road. A small manor house in limestone built in the early seventeenth century; the apple orchard, which is said to contain a descendant of the tree from which Newton saw the apple fall, still remains in front of the house. The principal rooms are on view at certain times.

BEATRIX POTTER

By Eleanor Graham

✧

IT is a strange story that lies behind the Beatrix Potter books – the story of a life begun in the chilliest, most cold-hearted, of Victorian households, all starch and pretentiousness bolstered up with nurses, governesses, butler, and coachmen with a lonely little girl living her orderly life in the forlorn isolation of a third-floor nursery in a Kensington house; and ending at Sawrey with a tough old lady going about her daily round in clogs with her skirts pinned back and a sack over her head, a successful farmer and (though too late for any cluster of children) a happy wife.

Good things, we all know, have come out of lonely childhoods. Beatrix Potter certainly suffered, but the solitude intensified a naturally vivid imagination, and in the long spells of quiet she re-lived her experiences, both real and imaginary, drawing from the actual her own shrewd conclusions, and developing the sound sense of values which all her books evince.

Real life for her, even from an early age, was the hard, simple life of country folk as she saw it on farms and in cottages in Scotland during the three months of each year when her father took a house in the country and transferred to it his entire household – blissful holidays when she was free to live in all her members. There she saw and felt the meaning behind household drudgery

Hill Top, NEAR SAWREY, LANCASHIRE

with its endless scouring, washing and mending, cooking and baking, the contriving inspired by necessity and love. She recognized its dignity, and her own heart was touched by the warmth of that family life so different from her own. She seems almost to have studied it, learning its pattern phrase by phrase. In every period of her life, her love and admiration for the homely arts are evident, and it is this way of life which she expresses in nearly all her books.

She had the seeing eye and a memory which retained the feeling of a moment as well as the reflection of a scene. In London, with few books, hardly any toys, and no companions with whom to share the raptures of discovery, she had little to divert her, and the intensity of her experiences remained intact, so that she was able to return and enter into them again, expanding and developing them in the light of her imagination – following the mice and rabbits beyond the point at which they had, in reality, disappeared from sight. Her private world was undoubtedly one of many mansions.

She had some of the qualities which made Fabre great. She had the patience, the willingness to watch and wait, the powerful observation which many children have but so soon lose in the swarm of new activities which crowd in upon them in the ordinary course of everyday life. Even as a child she would lie still and watchful by the hour in the fields, learning the lives of the tiny creatures who moved about the tufty roots of meadow-grass and wild flowers. She drew and painted – leaves, flowers, animals, skulls and bones, anything – but always earnestly, with a naturalist's care for accuracy of detail. At home she had a big Natural History to refer to and when fresh specimens failed, she drew from its plates. Later she was permitted to go to the Natural History Museum at Kensington, alone and unchaperoned, and there she drew passionately.

This was only part of the vivid secret life which went on behind those wide, bright eyes of hers and the tight-shut mouth. Eager, lively, curious, she made a good listener even for those days when little girls were expected to be seen and not heard, and the stories of family history which she heard from her Grandmother Potter and others probably affected her whole life. They seemed to her, even then, so important that she devised a trick of writing very small so that she could put them down as they were told, without drawing attention to what she was doing.

Her father was a barrister, too wealthy to care about practising; but Beatrix found to her pride that she came also from more interesting folk, 'from generations of Lancashire yeomen and weavers, obstinate, hard-headed, matter-of-fact folk, Puritans, Non-jurors, Dissenters'. They had been well known in the north and, in their own generations, as Unitarians, Radicals, Liberals : honest, thinking men, making their money in the mills and spending it on farms.

One of her grandmother's stories struck right home to the heart of the small girl who remembered it with special significance all her days. It described the grandmother as a little girl, driving with her father in a gig across Lancaster Sands under a rising moon, watching with great anxiety the incoming tide, for she carried a heavy bag of gold in her lap – gold with which to pay for another farm her father was buying.

'I hold that a strongly marked personality can influence descendants for generations,' Beatrix Potter wrote very late in her life. She had become a great believer in heredity, in 'breed', and put it to the test in her farming. As Mrs Heelis of Sawrey, she proved also that *she* had bred true to type, for she became renowned throughout the County as, in the words with which she had proudly described her ancestors, an *obstinate, hard-headed, matter-of-fact* woman with whom it was difficult to associate the long row of pretty little nursery books.

The loneliness of childhood in Kensington had been relieved by the attentions of three good women, a nurse of character, a kind governess, and, finally, by a gay young governess who married early and remained at hand, near enough for at least regular if not frequent visits in one of the less important of the family carriages. That governess became Mrs Moore and started a long family. To her children Beatrix Potter became something of a fairy godmother – and they were the means by which the spell of her dismal captivity was ultimately broken. For them she shaped into stories the fantasies with which she had lived so long, and drew the pictures which, in her books, have become as much a part of the inheritance of children everywhere as Hill Top Farm is of the whole nation.

The Tale of Peter Rabbit was first written in a letter with pictures in pen and ink for one of the Moore children during a long illness. It was not published until nine years later when Beatrix Potter was thirty-six, still cloistered in her nurseries and subject to her parents. She had become diffident, though quite untouched by bitterness or self-pity. She had given up some ambitions – notably to illustrate a serious work on fungi, for which she had filled albums at the Natural History Museum with exquisite, careful drawings. But she was no longer friendless. There was, for instance, Canon Rawnsley whom she had met during holidays (now mainly spent in the Lake District). He had encouraged her to make her little books, to try getting a publisher or, at worst, to print them herself. She did, in fact, print both *Peter Rabbit* and *The Tailor of Gloucester* privately before a publisher would have them.

Looked at in the light of her own circumstances, the published form of *Peter Rabbit* reveals itself as a great venture, anxiously undertaken. She was always confident of her ability to reach and please a child, but had no such faith to sustain her in facing the adult world; and she had now a publisher to satisfy and the buying public to attract. The careful simplicity of both text and drawings barely hides that tremulous anxiety to please. In her original letter to the sick child she had drawn the rabbit from one of her pets, a wild rabbit who had lived nine years in captivity and died just before she came to make the coloured pictures for the book. She had to substitute a new and younger rabbit as model, and the difference in colour and line worried her, as letters to her publisher show. Her background scenes were gathered from anywhere or nowhere – a tree from Keswick, Mr McGregor from Scotland, the potting-shed from her grandmother's house in Hertfordshire, the lily-pond from Wales.

In her nursery, she must often have watched the mice

come out from behind the wainscot to play. She draws them with such felicity, and always as good little creatures with their own natural dignity. The mice in *The Tailor of Gloucester* are enchanting creatures, and all her own, though the rest of the tale was one she had heard in the West Country about a tailor, a waistcoat, and *No more Twist*! With the care and thoroughness which were so characteristic of her, she sketched the old streets of Gloucester which were its proper setting, searched the cottages for the hearths and homes she wanted, found in Chelsea a tailor actually squatting on his bench in an old shop, just as she showed him in the book. She went to the Victoria and Albert Museum to copy the embroidery pattern from an old coat there. But for the mice she had only to set her fancy free, and this book is, indeed, a charming piece of self-expression, though actually written for a child, and she was, in fact, half afraid that it might appeal more to old ladies than children. In war-time editions it seemed to me that the street scenes had begun to fade a little, though the pretty, industrious, good-natured little mice and the pink-edged teacups are as fresh as when she first painted them.

She had, at last, a practical outlet for her mind, a stimulus for her ambition, and she was enjoying the satisfaction of accomplishing a set purpose. Her spirits rose and, with them, her courage, though her father was making himself exceedingly unpleasant over the whole business with his tantrums and scolding, detesting heartily anything which might promise her independence. The old obstinacy in the breed stood her in good stead now and, though for the sake of peace she had to beg

159

her publishers to say no more for the present of another book, she must have gone on working at it for *Squirrel Nutkin* came out in the same year as *The Tailor of Gloucester*. It sparkled with that brilliant inventiveness which had kept her spirit young and her mind alive throughout the long, drab years of her protracted childhood. She used an old repetitive pattern as the frame for this tale, and filled it with fun and gaiety: the enchanting ingenuity of the offerings made to Old Brown on each of the six days of the nutting, the impertinences of Nutkin, the cunning working in of old rhymes and riddles which all children of the day would know already – these show Beatrix Potter coming into her own. She had a particular feeling about bringing these old rhymes into her stories and expressed her thankfulness that the publishers did not want to cut them out.

Yet she was still not quite sure of herself, did not wholly trust her imagination, or believe how much more appreciated her own inventions would be than such borrowed notions as the squirrels' rafts.

The series was selling well. Even at a shilling a copy, they brought in a useful sum of money, and she suddenly realized that she could earn her own living.

Nevertheless, the two books she published in the following year gave little sign of that increased courage. One was a sequel to *Peter Rabbit*, and when it was done she felt she had used every conceivable rabbit situation and prayed she might never draw one again. The other book, *The Tale of Two Bad Mice*, is very different from any of her others, as though she had lost her good feeling for everything in its proper place, as though the dolls and

160

dolls' house had not been assimilated into her own personal fantasy – and indeed she had too little acquaintance with happy nursery life to be at home with them. Even the appearance of her two pets, Hunca Munca and Tom Thumb, does not put happiness into the tale: rather they introduce a tone of destructiveness which throws its own light on the conflict that was raging in the author's heart.

She was thinking of escape and freedom at that time, though her thoughts had as yet to be kept secret, and she knew she would have to fight every step of the way and to endure humiliating scenes with her parents.

She found herself on the one hand being drawn into an attachment to a member of her publishing house. At the same time, with her accumulating royalties, she had enough money to buy herself a haven – a farm to escape to.

By discussing the matter with her father as a form of investment not unusual in their family, she obtained his consent, and, in the following year, 1905, Hill Top Farm became hers. That she might have any thought of living there, or of running the farm herself, was too wildly preposterous in Mr Potter's eyes for a moment's serious consideration. Throughout the rest of her life, however, there are signs in plenty of what a sense of fulfilment, of added strength and purpose, its mere possession gave her.

That summer, in spite of all her parents could say, she accepted Mr Norman Warne's proposal of marriage. Before Christmas (before they could be married) he died. That was in her fortieth year – a strange year indeed – and what would she have done with the farm if she had married a London publisher?

The books of that remarkable year were the best she had yet done. A new vigour and self-confidence surged through them. She was happy; she was released. In *The Tale of Mrs Tiggywinkle* she described a former pet, 'the cleanest little creature' she had ever kept, and delightfully transformed it into the conscientious little washerwoman of the fells! The scene is not yet Sawrey, but on the other side of Derwentwater, near Catbells; and for the first time she drew her picture of that life to which she had given her heart when she was a little girl. There is the cottage kitchen of her dreams, rag rug before the gleaming range, the flagged floor, and the busy little creature working industriously, and taking pride in all she does. The promise of her own fulfilment is surely evident here.

In *The Pie and the Pattypan* appears Beatrix Potter's native brand of humour, a dry humour, poking gentle fun at genteel folk, chuckling over her own insight into the curious little ways of human nature, good-humoured, absolutely without sentimentality. Some at least of the effects on her of Mr Warne's death are to be seen in a comparison of these with the books which came after them.

Three books were published in the next year: *The Tale of Mr Jeremy Fisher* has certainly less vitality, though again the germ was ten years old, having appeared in another letter to the Moore children. It has not the sparkle of later books, nor the cosy warmth of *Mrs Tiggywinkle*, nor anything of the humour in *The Pie and the Pattypan*. The other two were the first in the smaller series, *The Fierce Bad Rabbit* and *Miss Moppet*, the story being no more than a caption to each picture and the drawings were bare, often with no background scene at all. Both might have been pot-boilers (in spite of an occasional dash of humour in the latter) – perhaps for extra money for Hill Top? Or they may have been done merely to keep her mind off heartbreak and disappointment. All three suggest a mind much preoccupied with other things. The other two of the small series came out several years later, in 1917 and 1922, and were a good deal more lively both in words and pictures, consisting of nursery rhymes, some traditional, some original. The best of all pictures of Mrs Tiggy appears in one of them, *Apply Dapply's Nursery Rhymes*.

Beatrix certainly suffered deeply at this time, but the farm remained to comfort her, and it brought about a new blooming of spirit in her. She still was not free to go and live there, but at this period her family usually took houses in the Lake District for their long summer holiday, and from them she made her way determinedly to and fro every day to Sawrey, travelling by whatever means of transport were available – a slow, gruelling journey as a rule.

Room by room she made the cottage her own. She planned and stocked the garden – the planning she could do, the year round, in London or anywhere else. Trusting to her own judgement – and wisely as it turned out – she put the former owner in as farm manager, and as she watched the development of her property in his capable hands, she began her own apprenticeship to the sort of life she had long loved and now most fervently desired to live.

She still found time to draw – indeed her books must

have acquired new significance in her eyes – and what she drew was Sawrey and the farm. She drew Hill Top as it stands to-day, with the garden and farmyard and its typical interior. She felt no need to look beyond the immediate present for inspiration, neither back to former pets or abroad for quaint notions. All trace of conflict disappeared out of her work, though she was still fast under the thumb of her father. A sense of the duty she owed them had been ground into her by her parents to bitter purpose and she could not disregard it. Each autumn she had to leave her cherished land, to return with them to London. Her health suffered during these periods of banishment and her imagination wandered always back to Sawrey.

She can no longer have had any doubt of her ultimate escape. Hill Top would one day be her home though the present frustration, particularly at her age, was hard to bear. In the meantime, she put new friends into possession, Tabitha Twitchett and Tom Kitten, the Puddle-ducks, Sam Whiskers, Pigling Bland – yes and even Messrs Tod and Brock. It should, perhaps, be said here that she never did live at Hill Top. Her ultimate emancipation included marriage, and Hill Top seemed too small for two. Besides, by then she had bought another farm, an adjoining property with a larger house in which she and her husband were to spend thirty happy years together. But she never ceased to cherish Hill Top as the realization of a long dream. She never changed or let the house.

The cream of her work lies in the books that followed, and they were rich with full fertility of mind and imagination, sparkling with originality, the new elasticity of spirit, and her own dry humour. They reflected most surely her mounting confidence, not only in herself but in life. She knew with certainty that she had found her own niche and purpose in life and was glad that her lines had fallen in such pleasant places. Her whole being was resolutely moving towards fulfilment.

The first of these books was *Tom Kitten* in which fantasy is secondary altogether to the reality of the background scene, though the invention is rich and gay. Miss Potter painted into these pages (and those of the other 'Sawrey' books) her own delight in her treasures. There in the frontispiece stands the little house itself, with gate, porch, and flower-bordered path up to the door. Through the later pages are pictures of the passage and the stairs, a deep window in one of the bedrooms, the farmyard and outhouses, the winding road disappearing over the hills. She peopled the house with cats, and, out of doors, introduced the Puddleducks, delicious, foolish neighbours, of whom more was to be heard in *Jemima Puddleduck*, a tale of the kind of everyday circumstances familiar to any country-bred child, with pictures which caught exactly the familiar expressions of farmyard creatures, the idiotic simplicity of ducks, the sagacity of sheepdogs – and, of course, the slyness of foxes. 'It does not do to be sentimental on a farm', wrote Miss Potter, in connexion with lambskin hearthrugs, and it is in this balance of mind that she finds the humour in commonplace things. She could even see the funny side of rats at Hill Top Farm, peculiarly destructive and pertinacious rats, which it took all her ingenuity and determination to outwit! She could laugh at the effrontery of Sam Whiskers (as she called the rat of Hill Top) sitting up in broad afternoon sunlight under the kitchen table to eat his dinner (certainly stolen from her larder), and he became as much a part of her life there as the mice behind the wainscot in the Kensington nurseries. So came *The Tale of Sam Whiskers*, also called *The Roly Poly Pudding*, with its delicious pictures of Sam stealing a pat of butter out of the dairy while his lean and anxious wife snatched a lump of dough out of the bread-pan, set before the fire to rise. Beatrix continued to give news of him for years afterwards to the many children all over the world to whom she wrote.

It is strange that she followed these books with *The Flopsy Bunnies* which told another tale of the Peter Rabbit family and departed from the Sawrey scene. It was written and illustrated while she was with her parents in Wales, and the change of theme is suggestive. What was going on between her and the tyrants? Could she not bear to dream for the moment of her loved Hill Top? Or did she merely yield to pressure from readers for a sequel to an old favourite? It is idle, of course, to speculate – yet that was another fateful year for her. The books continued to sell widely and increasingly. She was always surprised to see how much money they yielded; and she was preparing to buy her second farm. Moreover, the negotiations for the sale brought her into contact with the man she married four years later, William Heelis, the solicitor who put the deal through for her. Could this evidence of her absorption in Sawrey and farming have roused her father to fresh storms of protest?

It is easily seen that her joy in Hill Top had been somehow dimmed, for though she returned to Sawrey for her next book (published in the same year as the *Flopsy Bunnies*) it was not about the farm nor the house, but the village shop – and a deliciously shrewd, good-humoured picture of life on both sides of the counter it is in *Ginger and Pickles*. But in the next two books (and only one a year) she still avoids Hill Top, and goes down mouseholes again for *The Tale of Mrs Tittlemouse*, while in *Timmy Tiptoes*, a tale about grey squirrels, she turns abroad for her chipmunk and the bear. Each of them has its moments, but neither can stand beside the Hill Top books for originality or inventiveness.

Through these years Beatrix Potter suffered a great deal from influenza and its familiar depression, and was kept for weeks in bed with an affected heart. She was on the far side of forty-five, and the future must often have looked dark to her as she lay there, at the mercy of her parents. However, the connexion with William Heelis had 'taken'. It was he who kept her alive with news of Sawrey when she was ill. It was he who gave her the courage to take hold of life again. In 1912 she published *The Tale of Mr Todd*, a much longer story than usual which begins: 'I have made many books about well-behaved people. Now, for a change, I am going to make a story about two disagreeable people. ... Nobody could call Mr Todd nice. ... He had half a dozen houses but he was seldom at home.' The scene is round about Hill Top though the farm does not appear; the spirit makes it plain that the author was recovering.

Beatrix had to face the same bitter opposition from her

parents over her second offer of marriage. The Potters were 'Bar and Bench' and Mr Heelis only a country solicitor. Very reasonably she saw their objections but, as reasonably, made up her mind to accept the offer. She married William at St Mary Abbots, Kensington, in 1913 and brought out, in the same year, the last and in some ways the best of the Sawrey tales, *The Tale of Pigling Bland*. She had had it in mind all through these past years of depression, for in 1910 she had written: 'I think I shall put myself in my next book. It will be about pigs, and I shall put me walking about with my old sow, Goosie. She is such a pet!' And she did put herself into this 'Tale of a Christmas Pig'. It was the peak and climax of her literary work, cunningly bringing in old saws and rhymes about pigs, sparkling with delicious fun and rich with the country scene she loved so much. The characterization of the pigs is delicate and throughout there is an infectious welling-up of fun and gaiety. Pigs were an important feature of cottage economy at Hill Top. 'The whole district is planted out with my pigs,' she wrote, 'but we still take an interest in them because if they grow well, we shall *get a name for pigs*. Such is fame!'

If the Pig book was the climax, the finale came six years later in *The Tale of Johnny Town Mouse*, the old fable re-dressed to suit the circumstances, for Beatrix could at last count herself settled and at peace, and through the mouth of the Country Mouse she makes her farewell speech. Other books were to come, but she did not want to write or paint any more. She had become Mrs Heelis of Sawrey, the tough old lady successfully embarked on her late marriage and her late career as a farmer, going round her fields and byres in clogs, with her skirts pinned back and a sack over her head.

'"What do you do when it rains?" the town mouse asked Timmy Willie.

'"When it rains, I sit in my little sandy burrow and shell corn and seeds from my Autumn store. I peep out at the throstles and blackbirds on the lawn, and my friend Cock Robin. And when the sun comes out again, you should see my garden and the flowers – roses and pinks, and pansies – no noise except the birds and the bees, and the lambs in the meadows. ..."

'One place suits one person, another place suits another person. For my part I prefer to live in the country, like Timmy Willie.'

Hill Top, *Lancashire*

Behind the Tower Bank Arms, in the village of Near Sawrey, two miles south-east of Hawkshead. A seventeenth-century farmhouse to which Miss Potter made additions in her lifetime. The house, to which the public is admitted at certain times, is filled with a collection of her furniture, pictures, and books, besides some of the original drawings for her children's books.

BERNARD SHAW

By Hesketh Pearson

F EW, if any, famous men appear to have derived so
large a part of their natures from heredity and upbringing as Bernard Shaw, whose main characteristics
were directly traceable not only to his father and mother
but to the conditions in which his youth was passed. His
father was a comedian with a passion for anti-climax,
and not a little of Shaw's dramatic method was due to
his father's jokes. 'When I was a boy of only fourteen,'
said Shaw senior, 'my knowledge of swimming enabled
me to save your Uncle Robert's life.' Having duly impressed his son and heir with the necessity of learning
how to swim, he could not help adding: 'And to tell you
the truth I never was so sorry for anything in my life
afterwards.' He was a drunkard as well as a humorist,
and this cut him off from his relations, which again had
an effect on his son, whose early sense of being a social
outcast developed into a revolutionary attitude towards
society and gave him a fellow-feeling for other pariahs.

The mother's nature was utterly dissimilar from the
father's. She never made a joke in her life, and she did
not think her husband's frequent intoxication at all
funny. It is even doubtful whether she would have
laughed if he had fallen downstairs and broken his neck.
She frankly disliked him, displayed no affection for her
children, and retired into a world of her own, becoming

170

Shaw's Corner, AYOT ST LAWRENCE, HERTFORDSHIRE

independent of family ties, self-sufficient, and engrossed in singing and music. There was an atmosphere of kindliness and indifference in the home which helped to produce the G.B.S. who seemed to his acquaintances to have no domestic roots, no normal affections, no common feelings, and whose general benevolence was only equalled by his personal heartlessness. Beyond the home the social reformer was born. As a child he was taken out by a servant, who was supposed to perambulate the Dublin squares and other genteel spots, but who actually took him into the slums where her friends and relatives lived in dirty tenements and into public houses where the boozy clients were too familiar with him. Such experiences laid the foundations of his lifelong loathing of poverty and his stern desire to exterminate the poor.

What might have been anticipated from this loveless atmosphere, with its shiftless gentility and anarchic tendency, was the emergence of one whose development and success were directly due to his industry and purpose. Though Shaw detested the work, he was a model cashier in a land agent's office for four years from the age of sixteen. This was followed by nine years of penury in London, when he lived on his mother and learnt his profession as a writer by doggedly producing five long novels, all of which he hated, possibly because they were rejected by every publisher to whom he sent them. From the moment he discovered his objective in life as a Socialist his exertions became phenomenal. He spoke frequently at all sorts of places, indoors and outdoors, travelled all over the country, lecturing and debating, wrote innumerable tracts and articles, attended countless committee meetings, and meanwhile managed to earn his livelihood as a critic of books, painting, music, and the theatre. Then, as if his activities as a social reformer and journalist were not enough, he began to write plays. An almost unexampled capacity for work was therefore the chief feature of his character. He was constitutionally incapable of idling. On the rare occasions when he was doing what he described as nothing, careful inquiry would discover that he was developing photographs or studying phonetics or practising voice production or learning horticulture or peering through microscopes at bacteria or playing the piano. 'My rise to eminence was the effect of pure gravitation on my scriptorial industry,' he said. Again and again he worked until he was exhausted, and having revived he went at it once more with no decrease of energy. He throve on it, and would have died of boredom if he had ever taken what other people considered a pleasantly lazy holiday.

Next to his diligence the most noticeable aspect of his nature was a quality that almost seems to preclude assiduity, though Voltaire, his closest parallel in literature, was similarly endowed. Both of them worked like ants; yet neither could take life quite seriously, with the inevitable result that soberly serious people thought them insincere. Shaw's mental gaiety practically amounted to spiritual inebriety. He could no more help clowning than a born actor can help posing. His speeches were far more entertaining than any plays except his own. After keeping an audience enthralled with an impressive piece of eloquence, he would reduce the whole thing to absurdity with a quip and the preceding silence would be shattered

by a hurricane of laughter. There never was such a platform performer, and the famous political orators of his
age seemed barren and tawdry by comparison. His gaiety
infected his personality as thoroughly as his plays; and
his statement that he had to create a legendary character
in order to camouflage his natural timidity, that for the
purpose of obtaining a hearing he had to express his real
opinions with the utmost levity, was merely an attempt
to give a rational explanation for an irrational element in
his composition. There is a streak of insanity in genius
which expresses itself in folly, hilarity, buffoonery, irre-
sponsibility, or some such form of mental riot. Shakespeare, Swift, Johnson, Dickens: all exhibited it, but
Shaw more than any of them, because he had less ballast
than they and was less immersed in life.

Yet he was right in describing himself as constitutionally shy and timid, and without what someone called his
wonderful flow of vegetable spirits he would have felt
awkward in social intercourse. As it was, the man in
converse did not resemble the man in correspondence.
His letters were excessively candid, his manners extremely amiable, and one had the impression that Shaw
with a pen in his hand was arrogant while Shaw in talk
was diffident. He was the 'star' of the drama when alone
or standing before an audience, but in a drawing-room
he was merely a member of the cast. Also there was
nothing heroic or adventurous in his attitude to life. He
was cautious in all his dealings, pedantically legal-mind-
ed, as economical as an old maid, and as careful in
thought as he seemed reckless in expression. Nothing
was more remarkable about his career than the fact that

a man who appeared to be so outspoken so seldom gave offence. This was because he never committed himself to a statement that he could not substantiate and never said anything critical about a person without conveying a compliment, the very exaggeration of his stricture removing its sting. 'I assure you I was always, like Shakespeare, "a very civil gentleman",' he once told me. 'Even as a critic my attacks had something flattering implied which took the malice out of them. Ellen Terry, when the Henry Irvingites attacked me furiously, said that I was the only critic who had really done him justice.'

His inborn caution made him a first-rate man of business. With far more knowledge of law and economics than the theatre-managers and book publishers, he looked after their interests as well as his own, and always drafted the contracts he made with them. 'Will you sign or will you argue?' he asked Forbes-Robertson. Knowing his man, the actor signed without glancing at the contract. All the Repertory theatres blessed Shaw, for his percentages, unlike those of other leading playwrights, were reasonable, and he knew that a good contract is one that is good for both parties to it. Yet, though he made far more money than he ever wanted, he could have trebled his income if his preoccupation with writing and public work had not prevented him from attending to his own business until circumstances compelled him to do so. 'I should have taken a business partner with a flair for advertisement,' said the most widely advertised man in the kingdom. To save himself trouble he carefully cultivated a reputation for rapacity and meanness, which possibly halved his morning mail from beggars and considerably reduced his communications from money-lenders, betting-tipsters, and the army of folk who make their fortunes by relieving other people of theirs.

Curiously enough the man who became a symbol for everything called modern was in most respects very old-fashioned. His manners were courtly, his prose style was classical, his philosophy was pre-Darwinian, his habits were regular, his behaviour was conventional, his home-life was humdrum, his whole existence was conducted with propriety; and all this is reflected in his plays, which are notable for their traditionalism. When they first appeared the critics thought them wildly original and undramatic in form, the players thought them completely lacking in good 'acting' parts, and the audiences did not know what to think. But apart from the genius inseparable from their creator, they display the technique of Euripides and Molière, the idiosyncratic differentiation of character seen in Shakespeare, and the long rhetorical speeches which are a leading feature of primitive dramaturgy.

Consistency was another of his virtues, though many people thought it a vice. He had the unyielding temperament of a totalitarian. What he had said in his twenties he was still saying in his nineties. Having once fixed his point of view, he stuck to it through thick and thin. 'Never argue: repeat your assertion' was his motto in life. Consequently, whenever he debated in public with eminent contemporaries like G. K. Chesterton and Hilaire Belloc, he took little notice of their philosophy but continued to reiterate his own. He was a mental acrobat, but whether standing on his legs or his head the same expressions issued from his mouth. The drawback to this sort of temperament is that whatever does not harmonize with the totalitarian's point of view has to be attacked, not on sensible human grounds but because it is at variance, not on account of its faults but of its difference. Because the plays of Ibsen were in sympathy with Shaw's mental attitude, the plays of Shakespeare, which did not conform with their outlook, had to be ridiculed. When he described the Elizabethan playwright Chapman as 'a really great literary figure', I reminded him that as a dramatic critic he had called Chapman 'a blathering unreadable pedant' who wrote 'balderdash'. He was not in the least taken aback. 'When I had to smash Bardolatry in the lump,' he said, 'I had to fight so foully that any critic can disqualify me by a few quotations.' There was no earthly reason why he should have had to smash Bardolatry in the lump. No one except a few cranks like Swinburne was taking the least interest in the minor Elizabethan dramatists. But Shaw was carrying on a campaign to obtain recognition for Ibsen, not to mention himself, and every dramatist whose philosophy of life could not be wrested into agreement with theirs had to be laid low, irrespective of merit. We have lived to see the same foul fighting in totalitarian politics.

To implant his doctrines firmly and make them acceptable socially Shaw had to cultivate a manner, and in this respect he was right in saying that he had to become an actor in public life, though the histrionic bent was there before he developed it. Impatient by nature, he had to learn how to appear, and to be, unruffled. It was of the utmost importance to him that the Fabian Society should not suffer from the bickerings, disagreements, and jealousies that eventually wrecked all the other Socialist societies; and so he painfully acquired a self-control which seemed to others almost inhuman. He drudged away on numberless committees and sub-committees, gave years of his life to work for which he could receive no credit, yet never once lost his temper or showed irritation, though often enough his fellow-workers were raging around him. As a personality, this was the most remarkable feat of his career; and though his equanimity sometimes infuriated less bridled souls, it was generally admitted that but for him the Fabian Society would have gone the way of H. M. Hyndman's Federation, Stewart Headlam's Guild, and William Morris's League.

That Shaw had a deal of the actor in his nature, apart from what he assumed for diplomatic purposes, could be fully appreciated only by those who saw him producing his own plays. He knew exactly how every part should be performed, and instead of bullying an actor with useless criticism would go up on to the stage and do the whole thing himself, purposely exaggerating the effect he wished to obtain so as to prevent the actor from copying him, burlesquing his own creations in order to clarify them and inspire the players with self-confidence. In this way he gave his characters the vividness of caricature and brought every part to life by the vigour of his impersonation. To watch him darting about the stage, clowning the creatures of his imagination, misquoting their lines, inventing comic 'business' as he went along, and roaring with laughter at his own antics, was an experience that no actor in his company would have missed. The atmosphere of friendliness and informality at his rehearsals was, I fancy, unique in the history of the London stage. In illustration of this: at one rehearsal he advised a thoroughly experienced player to pass behind the table at a particular moment; at the next rehearsal he advised him to pass in front of it. 'But, Mr Shaw, you told me yesterday to go behind the table.' 'Oh, did I? Well, that just shows the danger of paying any attention to what I say.' The actors agreed that rehearsals under Shaw's direction were very entertaining: he had the exceptional gift of making work seem like a hobby.

Of hobbies in the ordinary sense he had none, unless the energy he put into photography may be described as such. He played no games, and attempts to make him do so usually ended with a display of irritation by his opponent, because he did not care whether he won or lost and never bothered to count the scores. He enjoyed walking and swimming and motoring merely for the pleasure of the exercise, and at one time he practised boxing for the same reason; but when Eugene Sandow wanted to take him as a pupil and develop his muscles, Shaw said: 'You misunderstand my case. I have seen you supporting on your magnificent chest twenty men, two grand pianos and a couple of elephants. But my object as to pianos and elephants and crowds is to keep them off my chest, not to heap them on to it.' Shaw also had a secret exercise: he sang, every night before he went to bed, from operas, oratorios, cantatas, whatever was singable, whether soprano, contralto, tenor, or bass. No one ever knew of this except his mother, his wife, and his domestic staff.

Though he gave and accepted hospitality, he seldom attended social gatherings for men only, because 'men would not enjoy themselves decently in the absence of women,' he informed me. 'There was a male party in the house of a friend in Westminster at which I sat next Gilbert Chesterton. After dinner they began throwing bread at one another; and one of them began making smutty speeches. They were actually drunk enough to expect a contribution from me. I got up and went home. ... When I first saw an assembly of respectable and sober English ladies and gentlemen going Fantee, and behaving like pirates debauching after a capture, I was astounded. I am used to it now; but it is not possible for me to take part in such orgies.' Socially Shaw was a very charming companion, even his vanity being of an inoffensive kind, though it resulted in so many portraits and busts that H. G. Wells complained it was not possible to move about Europe without seeing him everywhere in oils or effigy. Friends continually tempted him to dine or lunch with them, his refusals being couched in humorously violent terms; and when he did accept an invitation to a restaurant he made it clear that he was interested neither in the food nor in the company but in the economics of the place.

Which brings us to another of his outstanding traits: an insatiable curiosity. He collected information about everything, as another man would collect stamps or coins or eggs. Whenever he met someone who had made a special study of machinery or advertising or voice production or stained glass or medicine or aeronautics or typography or indeed anything, he pumped that expert dry and stored up whatever knowledge might be useful to him in the future. He could not pass a pneumatic drill in the street without stopping to find out how it worked and to note the result. He would discuss the pruning of trees with his gardener as keenly as the state of his nerves with a neurologist. He was abreast of every scientific discovery of his time, and engaged in controversy with the leading scientists, many of whom were furious that a layman should not only know as much of the subject as themselves, but often get the better of them in debate, and be in a position to ridicule their pet theories. In short, his interests were without limit, and will only be fully apparent to the world when his correspondence is collected a century hence. It will be the most various, voluminous, and amusing collection in literature, and future generations will wonder how he had found time for any activity but the writing of letters.

Shaw's Corner, Hertfordshire

At the south-west end of the village of Ayot St Lawrence. A red-brick house built in the early part of the twentieth century, with a summer-house in the garden in which G. B. S. did much of his writing in recent years. There was no public access during his life-time, but Shaw's Corner is to be maintained as a literary shrine.

George Stephenson's Cottage, WYLAM–ON–TYNE, NORTHUMBERLAND

GEORGE STEPHENSON

By Mary Winser

AMONG George Stephenson's papers there is preserved a receipt for a payment from the Reverend H. G. Liddell for 'teaching and instructing his son Charles Liddell in the trade, business or occupation of a civil engineer from the 17th day of June 1834 for the term of four years'. Charles Liddell was the brother of Dean Liddell of Christ Church, Oxford, and uncle therefore of the Alice who went through the looking-glass to make one of the strangest of all railway journeys, in the company of a gentleman dressed in white paper, a beetle, and a goat.

It is good to find even so slight a link between Alice and George Stephenson, since between them they did so much for the enjoyment of children. As founder of the railway system, Stephenson changed the face of the landscape, and was responsible for an enormous increase in the wealth of the country. (Lewis Carroll's looking-glass travellers were not exaggerating much when they cried out that the smoke of the engine was worth a thousand pounds a puff.) But equally beyond all calculation is the amount of pleasure Stephenson's work has given to all small boys who dream of driving engines, to the scattered brotherhood of train-watchers at the end of the platform, and to everyone who has discovered that to put a couple of halfpennies on the railway line and watch a train run over them is to get the best enjoyment a penny can buy.

Stephenson was not the inventor of the locomotive, any more than he was the originator of the railway as such. Horses had hauled coal-wagons along wooden railroads for years before he was born, and by the beginning of the nineteenth century iron railroads were quite common in the collieries. Other men, Trevithick, Hackworth, and Blenkinsop among them, had made locomotives before Stephenson; their designs were available for him to improve on. But he was the only man among all the early locomotive inventors whose brain could compass the grand idea of an engineering scheme and carry it through down to the last detail. At a time when the manufacturers and coal-owners of the north were slowly beginning to realize the possibilities of the railway, Stephenson had the personality to win them over to the experiment, and the ability to provide, not locomotives only, but working railway systems that showed a profit to their owners.

George Stephenson was born in the village of Wylam near Newcastle on the 9th June 1781. Among the earliest things he must have seen were the loaded coal-wagons passing along the wooden railway outside his parents' cottage from the mine where his father worked as a fireman. George was the second of six children, and as his father earned only twelve shillings a week, there was no money to spare for their schooling; George went to work at the age of eight, pulling turnips for fourpence a day.

Engines had always fascinated him from the time when

as a small boy he used to make models of the coal-mine machinery out of clay. When he became assistant fireman to his father, at the age of fourteen, and later, when he had charge of a pumping engine himself, he learned everything his hands and eyes could teach him about the machinery, taking it to pieces in his spare time and studying every detail of its construction. At eighteen he learned to read, and had his first lessons in mathematics from the village schoolmaster; from that time onwards he read everything he could find on engineering, and particularly anything that had to do with steam engines. Ideas for building a locomotive of his own were forming in his brain for a long time before he had a chance of putting them into practice. For years yet he was known to the miners only as a cheerful companion, a young man who had a way with recalcitrant colliery engines, and a champion at throwing the hammer.

In 1802 Stephenson married Fanny Henderson, a maid in the farmhouse at Black Callerton where he lodged. A year later, in November 1803, their son Robert was born. From the first, Stephenson was determined to give his son the education he himself had missed, and in order to save the money for Robert's schooling he took on any extra work that came to hand – from unloading ballast from the Newcastle coal-ships to mending his neighbour's clocks and watches and cobbling their shoes.

Stephenson's promotion to engine-wright at the Killingworth colliery near Newcastle in 1812, at a salary of £100 a year, enabled him to send Robert to the village school and later to study mathematics at Mr Bruce's school in Newcastle. When the boy came home from school in the evening, he frequently went over his day's work with his father, and together they studied engineering plans and mechanical problems, sometimes making models of the inventions Stephenson found described in his books. This was the foundation of the famous partnership between George Stephenson and his son, who was to become his chief assistant and greatest successor in the work of railway building.

As engine-wright at Killingworth, in charge of all the colliery machinery, Stephenson was at last able to realize his dreams of building a locomotive which should replace the horses used for hauling coal-wagons on the colliery railway. He managed to persuade Lord Ravensworth, the principal partner, and uncle of the Charles Liddell who later became his apprentice, to provide the money needed, and in 1814 his first 'travelling engine', the 'Blucher', was completed. Slow and cumbrous as it was, the 'Blucher' had one very important feature – a device which had been employed by Trevithick but was ignored by later designers until Stephenson re-invented it. Largely to get rid of the noise made by the steam escaping from the cylinders, which it was feared might terrify all the cattle within earshot, Stephenson piped the steam into the chimney of the engine, thereby increasing the draught, and the combustion in the furnace, so that the power of the engine was almost doubled. Samuel Smiles, Stephenson's famous biographer, described the device in glowing terms: –

'This simple but beautiful expedient was really fraught with the most important consequences to railway communication; and it is not too much to say that the success of the locomotive has in great measure been the result of its adoption.'

Stephenson made a number of locomotives during the next few years, but though they satisfied the Killingworth coal-owners they aroused no interest in the world beyond the collieries. Few people at that time had any conception that the locomotive might one day supplant the canal barge or outpace the stage-coach. Even Edward Pease, a Darlington coal-owner who had realized the advantages and possibilities of the railroad, had only bargained for carriages drawn by 'men and horses or otherwise' on his proposed line from Darlington to Stockton-on-Tees, for which he obtained an Act of Parliament in 1821, in the face of stiff local opposition. Stephenson was appointed engineer of the line, and it was due to his persistence alone that a clause was added to the Railway Bill authorizing the use of locomotives for goods and passenger traffic. The revised Bill became law in 1823, and in the same year Stephenson opened a locomotive factory at Newcastle in the name of his son Robert, who had by then just completed a year at Edinburgh University.

In this, the first locomotive works in the world, Stephenson invested £1000, which had been presented to him for the invention of a miners' safety lamp. This lamp, which embodied the same principle as Sir Humphry Davy's safety lamp, was actually made and tested by Stephenson a week or so before Sir Humphry Davy delivered his famous lecture on the subject to the Royal Society in November 1815. The safety lamp was the most famous of Stephenson's inventions not connected with railways; and though there was later an outcry at an unknown engineer laying claim to the capabilities of one of the most distinguished scientists of the day – a claim that Stephenson himself never made – there is no doubt that the two inventions were made quite independently of one another.

Five locomotives were ordered from the Stephenson works for the Stockton and Darlington line, which was eventually opened in 1825. Its immediate success surpassed even Edward Pease's hopes, and its popularity with merchants, coal-owners, and above all with the passengers, did a great deal of good to Stephenson's reputation as an engineer. When the projectors of a railway between Manchester and Liverpool began their search for an engineer to superintend the construction of the line, it was to Stephenson that they came.

The Liverpool–Manchester Railway scheme aroused considerable interest, and equally bitter opposition. Angry farmers, fearful of the harm a railway line with its snorting, smoking locomotives might do to their crops and cattle, ordered the surveyors off their land and smashed their instruments with sticks and stones. The owners of the canal companies were no less alarmed for their monopoly of the goods transport between the two cities than were the local land-owners for the sanctity of their coverts, or the owners of the stage-coaches for the prosperity of their business. When the Railway Bill was brought before a Committee of the House of Commons in 1825, these opponents engaged the best men they could to speak against it.

It was Stephenson's task to prove to the Committee

that the scheme was from an engineer's point of view sound and practicable, and that in the teeth of the scepticism of the best engineers of the day. He said afterwards that the thing he found hardest in justifying the claims of his locomotives was to keep them down to a speed of ten miles an hour. The Directors of the railway were desperately anxious lest he should tell the Committee, what he himself believed, that his engines would easily travel at double the rate. During his cross-examination Stephenson's north-country speech was jeered at, his sanity questioned, and his whole project dismissed as absurd. This was particularly galling in view of the absurdity of many of the questions that were put to him; but sometimes he gave as good as he got. When asked whether horses and cattle would not be terrified by the sight of the smoking engine with its red-hot chimney, he replied, 'How would they know it wasn't painted?' Again he was asked 'Suppose now, that a cow were to stray upon the line and get in the way of the engine; would not that, think you, be a very awkward circumstance?'

'Yes,' was the famous retort, 'very awkward – *for the coo!*'

Stephenson was not to be shaken in his defence of the locomotives; but nothing would convince the Committee that the railway line itself could be laid in the way proposed; in particular it was held to be impossible to lay a line over the stretch of peat bog known as Chat Moss, where the spongy ground would scarcely bear the weight of a man. 'No engineer in his senses would attempt it', was the verdict of the experts; and the Bill was thrown out in consequence.

Stephenson was bitterly disappointed that this battle, which he had fought almost single-handed, had ended in defeat; but the directors of the railway company did not give up hope. A new survey of the line was made, and when the Bill was again presented to Parliament in the following year, it went through successfully. Stephenson was immediately appointed principal engineer, and work on the line began.

The first problem to be tackled was that of crossing Chat Moss. All attempts to drain the bog had failed, and to dig down through the mass of decaying mosses to the firm bottom twenty feet or so beneath was out of the question. Stephenson solved the difficulty by floating the line on a causeway of piled-up branches and hurdles, thatched with bundles of heather and topped with a layer of gravel on which the rails were laid.

It was only the first of any number of so-called impossibilities to which Stephenson had to find a solution during the four years which the railway took to build. The amount he did was heroic; not only had he to devise all the engineering work himself, with only a small staff to help him, but he had also to organize the labours of the large numbers of men employed on the line, many of whom were necessarily untrained, since the work they were to do was often of a kind never before attempted. One of his hardest tasks must have been to satisfy the directors of the company that their money was not being thrown away while bridges were built, tunnels and embankments made and miles of track laid down.

What tried him particularly was that many of the directors were still unwilling to use locomotives on the

192

railway at all, preferring the kind of stationary engine used in the collieries for dragging wagons along by the use of ropes. At last, however, the company was persuaded to offer a prize of £500 for the best locomotive weighing not more than six tons and able to drag a twenty-ton load on the level at ten miles an hour, to perform before them by the 1st October 1829.

Robert Stephenson had been out of England for most of the time that the Liverpool–Manchester railway was being built; but he came home in time to watch over the building of the locomotive which his father was entering for the competition. Five engines eventually appeared for the famous trial at Rainhill: a horse-drawn contraption called the 'Cycloped' submitted by one of the directors, which was immediately disqualified; the dainty-looking 'Novelty', which was first favourite with the spectators; the 'Perseverance'; George and Robert Stephenson's 'Rocket'; and Timothy Hackworth's 'Sanspareil', which today stands beside the 'Rocket' in the Science Museum in South Kensington.

The 'Rocket' – how strange to think that the result of the trial could ever have been in doubt! – was the only engine to satisfy the requirements of the contest and to perform its trial without breaking down. Where the directors had demanded a speed of ten miles an hour, the 'Rocket' travelled at an average rate of fifteen, and touched twenty-nine miles an hour on one of her trips. When, at the end of her trial, one of the directors who had most stoutly opposed the use of the locomotive lifted up his hands and exclaimed with the fervour of an Old Testament prophet, 'Now has George Stephenson at last delivered himself!', the future of the locomotive was assured.

John Dixon, who had been assistant surveyor to Stephenson on the Stockton and Darlington railway, wrote an enthusiastic account of the Rainhill trials to his brother, describing the 'Rocket' as 'by far the best engine I have ever seen for Blood and Bone united'. It was then inevitable to think of a locomotive in terms of a horse. Fanny Kemble, who was taken over the Liverpool and Manchester line some months before its opening, wrote of the engine as a 'snorting little animal which I felt rather inclined to pat', noting that 'they make these curious little fire-horses all mares'. Her letter continued with a description of George Stephenson himself, 'the master of all these marvels, with whom I am most horribly in love. ... His face is fine, though careworn, and bears an expression of deep thoughtfulness; his mode of explaining his ideas is peculiar and very original, striking, and forcible. ... He has certainly turned my head.'

A considerable ceremony marked the opening of the railway on 15th September 1830. Eight trains, their decorated carriages filled with the directors of the company and their guests, who included the Duke of Wellington, Sir Robert Peel, and Mr Huskisson, travelled from Liverpool to Manchester and back, passing crowds of enthusiastic spectators at every bridge and cutting along the route. The arrangements for the journey, and for the refreshments prepared for the travellers at Manchester, had been made with great care, and were set out with a certain finesse in the company's Orders of the Day; it is even recorded that 'before leaving the Refreshment

Rooms a Blue Flag will be exhibited as a signal for the Ladies to resume their Cloaks'.

The Orders of the Day had also asked the passengers not to leave their carriages while the engines halted on the way to take in water. Mr Huskisson, however, stepped out in order to speak to the Duke of Wellington, and was knocked down by a passing train; and although his carriage was immediately rushed to Manchester by a locomotive driven by George Stephenson himself, he died later that evening. Huskisson's accident made a sad ending to the day; but even in describing the tragedy Samuel Smiles took time to record that the engine that took Huskisson on to Manchester travelled at the rate of thirty-six miles an hour, and that this 'incredible speed burst upon the world with the effect of a new and unlooked-for phenomenon'. Very soon it was a phenomenon no longer; the Railway Age had begun.

Six years after the opening of the Liverpool and Manchester line there were over 11,000 miles of railway in the world, and engines were snorting along in many parts of Britain, bearing triumphant names. A list of the locomotives in use in the early 1830s on Robert Stephenson's Leicester and Swannington railway alone included a 'Phoenix', a 'Samson', an 'Elephant', a 'Goliath', a 'Leopard', a 'Mastodon', and a 'Pelican'.

George Stephenson, who was now thought of as one of the country's foremost engineers, built a number of railways during the next ten years, among them the Manchester and Leeds, the North Midland, and the Grand Junction Railway; but the Liverpool and Manchester railway remains his most famous achievement.

His judgement was unaffected by the sudden enthusiasm for the railway which followed on the general scepticism he had had to fight for so long. He held aloof from the wave of speculation that culminated in the 'Railway Mania' of the 1840s, and refused always to give his name to any railway enterprise unless he was convinced that it was sound from an engineering point of view, and likely to show an honest profit for the shareholders. He, who had for so long defended the railway and the locomotive from charges of absurdity, now defended them against impossible claims on their capacity, meeting ideas for switchback gradients and atmospheric railways, which enjoyed a short-lived popularity, with a dogged, hardheaded 'It won't do!'

Towards the end of his life, Stephenson, when Robert was building railways up and down the country, was occupied more with the business of his collieries and lime-works. In 1845 he twice visited Belgium, where he was received by the King of the Belgians and fêted by the Belgian railway engineers. Later in the year he went to Spain to examine the site of a proposed railway, and on the way home was taken ill with pleurisy, from which he never entirely recovered his strength.

He now spent most of his time at his home at Tapton, near Chesterfield, where he delighted to entertain his friends, particularly those who had known him as a young man. The garden at Tapton was famous for its melons and cucumbers, and Stephenson would show them off to his guests with the same cheerful pride with which he had once confided to a friend long before, when he had saved his first guinea, that 'he was now a rich man'. Conversation with his friends was always more pleasant to him than reading, and he frequently surprised even those who knew him best with his wide practical knowledge, the originality of his ideas, and his vigour in phrasing them. He would discuss clock making and surveying with engineers, and embroidery with ladies; and enlivened one meeting of railway directors, who were heartily sick of discussing nothing but railways, with an extempore lecture on birds' nests. All his knowledge and achievements did not cancel out the energetic simplicity of his character, or the boyishness of his nature which sent him out birds'-nesting in the spring and nutting every autumn.

Stephenson died after a short illness on 12th August 1848, almost exactly three years after the death of Elizabeth, his second wife, whom he had married in 1820.

One of his biographers gave to Stephenson the title of 'Father of Railways', and it suited him well. Certainly his appearance was patriarchal, to judge by the strong, dignified figure and wise countenance of John Lucas's portrait. The young men he trained as his assistants and lodged in his own house later became, many of them, railway builders themselves, developing the work that he had begun. But more important, the title recalls the human calibre of the great engineer. Stephenson's railways would never have been built if his gifts as an inventor had not been matched with the power to make other people believe in his work, and to direct them in carrying out his ideas. His workmen admired the way he went at every problem with the cheerful energy of his watchword: 'Persevere!' 'I never saw him in a hurry or bustle,' said one of them. 'He was generally in an attitude to talk and listen to somebody else.' Famous men admired him, his assistants were devoted to him. Nor is it surprising, since railway engines are the most majestic and lovable of all mechanical creatures, that the father of railways and the maker of the 'Rocket' should have been such a great and lovable man.

George Stephenson's Cottage, Northumberland

By the side of the railway, half a mile north-east of Wylam-on-Tyne toll bridge. A plain stone-built workman's cottage, *c.* 1750. There is no admission to the interior.

Smallhythe Place, TENTERDEN, KENT

ELLEN TERRY

By Harcourt Williams

❖

IN a glass case in the Shakespeare Memorial Museum at Stratford-upon-Avon is a letter addressed by Charles Kean to his stage manager, Mr Ellis. Thus it goes: 'Have the two Misses Terry – Kate and Ellen – at rehearsal of the Episode on Tuesday morning at eleven o'clock. I shall make use of both of them.'

That last prophetic phrase, 'I shall make use of both of them', is interesting because in her autobiography Ellen Terry speaks of herself repeatedly as a useful actress. That was indeed, she affirms, the limit of her ambition, albeit her genius took the matter out of her hands and established her as the leading actress of her day when she stood beside Henry Irving at the Lyceum Theatre.

Her story has been told many times, but never more happily than in her own exquisite telling. She was born at Coventry, in 1848, and for many years two houses in Market Street claimed to be the authentic birthplace. Now the rivalry has been finally resolved by the devastation of war. She was always a great home-maker. She collected cottages as some people collect old china – like Mark Antony's realms and islands, they were as plates dropped from her pocket! First there was The Firs, Gustard Wood, near Wheathampstead, Hertfordshire, where her two children were born – Edith Ailsa Craig

201

and Edward Gordon Craig. The house was designed by
Edward William Godwin, FSA.

It was in a lane near by that the famous chance meeting with Charles Reade took place, which led to Ellen
Terry's return to the theatre, thus giving to the world a
measure of beauty which otherwise it might never have
enjoyed.

The two children had the inestimable advantage of
spending their blossoming years in the historic and romantic surroundings of Hampton Court. One may read
of them doing bits from *As You Like It* in the Wilder-
ness with their mother for audience. They were always
ready to show visitors the sights – especially the young
trees which the gardeners had christened after her parts.
A silver birch was Iolanthe, a maple Portia.

Much of Ellen Terry's work at the Lyceum was done
from a house with a conventional exterior in Barkston
Gardens. It was chosen because it was near where her
mother lived, and doubtless it was convenient enough
during those momentous, laborious days; but cottages –
homes of escape into the country – began to make their
appearance. There was the Audrey Arms at Uxbridge,
of which I have heard the legend that by the terms of the
lease, Ellen Terry was obliged to serve ale on an 'off
licence' to any customer who came knocking at the
door.

Then there was Vine Cottage in the Kingston Vale.
One was able to feed the deer over the garden wall
which abutted on Richmond Park. I don't think there
was a vine, but there was certainly a tall monkey-puzzle
tree, so dear to Victorians, in the front garden. Vine

Cottage had the advantage of being within a cab drive of the Lyceum and Wellington Street. Ellen Terry took me there one day not long before she gave it up. I still possess a finely bound copy of Bacon's Essays and a bronze bust of Shakespeare small enough to go in the pocket, which she gave me on that occasion. She was a rare one to give, and she gave in such a way that the gift stayed in the memory – as well as in the pocket. Shakespeare and Bacon – strange bedfellows! Cryptograms and the like? No, I am sure there was no such stuff in her thoughts.

To the public of the eighteen-nineties, Tower Cottage, Winchelsea, was probably better known than the others, for about that time an illustrated interview with the actress appeared in the *Strand Magazine*, then at the height of its Sherlock Holmes popularity.

The cottage stands in a romantic position at the southeast corner of the ancient little town looking over the marshes to the sea and the church-crowned roofs of Rye. The garden is held up, as it were, by a stalwart wall beneath which the steep hill descends from one of the remaining towered gates that straddle the highway. That massive wall bedecked with stonecrop and fern is to be seen in the background of Millais' picture 'The Huguenot'. Gordon Craig, whose draughtsmanship was to lead him away from a stage career, designed one of his beautiful bookplates for his mother's home, embodying a map of Winchelsea with its rectangular streets – based, some say, on the Roman Camp. In that *Strand* article there is a sketch of Ellen Terry driving in a dog-cart to Winchelsea station. She loved driving, especially in high dog-carts which over-topped the hedges.

Many years later one dusky evening – that was the time of day she liked for such expeditions – she drove my wife along the narrow roads edged with reedy dykes round about Smallhythe. It was an exhilarating if some-what alarming experience, for the pace was a spanking one, while the driver, holding the reins lightly, kept her eyes mostly upon Jean as she sang her snatches of old songs and told her tales of friends and romantic lovers. There was no real danger, however, for Ellen Terry knew her country and her horse.

One afternoon – before the days of motors – she drove Henry Irving from Winchelsea to Tenterden Town. The road lay across the marshes by Camber Castle, through Rye, up the hill to Iden (Jack Cade met his end, says Shakespeare, in Iden's Garden), across the Rother and up over Oxney Island to Smallhythe Tollgate, which at that time still extorted dues from travellers. While waiting for the leisured opening of the white gates, Ellen Terry's eye must have rested, possibly for the first time, on a typical Kentish farm building of half-timber with over-hanging upper storey.

The long line of the red-tiled roof sheltering the weather-worn beams and plaster seemed to have become part of the landscape with the passing years. It was a case of love at first sight, and in the course of time she pos-sessed it. Of that drive to Tenterden on 14th August 1890 she wrote in her diary, 'Saw Clowes Marionettes'. Later, in *The Story of My Life* she tells how 'Henry saw one of Clowes's playbills in a shop window, but the per-formances only took place in the evening. He found out the proprietor and asked him what were the takings for a good night. The man said five pounds. Henry asked him if he would give a special show for that sum. He was delighted. Henry and I and my daughter Edy, and Fussie (the famous fox-terrier that was given to Ellen Terry by Fred Archer) sat in solemn state in the empty tent and watched the show, which was most ingenious and clever. Ever since that "command" performance, there have been two extra lines on the bills – "Patronized by Henry Irving and Ellen Terry".'

The purchase of the Smallhythe Farm was, I understood, not a great extravagance, for the accompanying acres were more sought after than the house itself – no housing shortage then, and old buildings built by craftsmen who delighted in their work were not appreciated then as they are to-day – and Ellen Terry was able to resell part of the land at a figure which covered much of her original outlay. Though generous to a fault, she was no spendthrift.

Charles Reade once said of her that she was as hard as nails in money matters. He thought that at the time of her return to the theatre when she was in desperate financial straits. She was in her early twenties, with two small children on her hands, and the brokers in the house! She should have been praised and not blamed for a certain shrewdness. Charles Reade, indeed, did come to change his opinion. He was a true friend to her, and in her work a sound adviser. His analysis of her beauty has become a classic: 'Ellen Terry is an enigma. Her eyes are pale, her nose rather long, her mouth nothing in particular. Complexion a delicate brickdust, her hair, rather like tow. Yet somehow, she is *beautiful*. Her expression *kills* any pretty face you see beside her. Her figure is lean and bony; her hand masculine in size and form. Yet she is a pattern of fawn-like grace. Whether in movement or repose, grace pervades the hussy.' What surprises me about the above, is that Charles Reade does not mention a certain flatness at the end of the nose, which made the whole face enchanting and incomparable.

Early experiences while touring with her parents when pay packets were small had taught her the value of money. In common with many successful artists, her pension list was secret but considerable. But she was astute and in many ways a good business woman. She was never one who cared to live extravagantly herself. There is an anecdote told of her during the 1914 war. She was scolding her housekeeper for using too many eggs. 'What is an egg, Miss Terry?' 'An egg is fourpence halfpenny, and don't you forget it.'

The farm at Smallhythe became hers about 1901. I think it was the home that was dearest to her heart, and when she first viewed it over the white gates by the tollhouse, she was looking at the windows of the room where some thirty-eight years later she was to die. Had the choice been in her hands she could hardly have found a lovelier or more peaceful spot.

When she moved in, she was still acting at the Lyceum though making occasional excursions to other theatres. One was to Stratford-upon-Avon. She came down to play Queen Katharine in Frank Benson's production of *Henry VIII* for the 1902 Festival Season. It was then that I first met her. Someone said of me at that time, that I seemed to be the happiest man in the world. Well, I was!

Just out of my teens, I was playing important parts in a repertory of Shakespeare's plays, and I was in daily contact with a woman I had adored for seven long years of boyhood. I know I was but one of thousands, and did not George Bernard Shaw say that there was no famous man of her period who was not in love with Ellen Terry? Certainly, I was not famous, but I so gladly shared their fate.

How helpful she was to us youngsters – how gracious. Such little things stick in my memory – perhaps they may add a touch to the background against which that incomparable woman shows like a spray of blossom. A tea-party at Marie Corelli's – Marie greeting her guest at the door with a rather theatrical curtsey of adulation. 'Ah, yes,' says Ellen Terry, taking her in her arms, 'but what about those nasty things you've been saying about us actors!' ...

At a reception given at the Memorial Theatre, a word of warning in my ear when Clement Scott, the celebrated critic, said something about my acting. 'Make use of it, if you like, but don't value it too high.' ... I remember her standing, drawn to her full height, by the jamb of the door to say good-bye to me. Her shoulders (so lovely in themselves) held firmly against the wall; an attitude that gave her whole body the poise and serenity of some cathedral saint. A few moments before she had taught me a little lesson. I had told her a story of Frank Rodney which turned on his bad complexion. Certainly that fine actor would tell it against himself, but as I made the point of the story, Ellen Terry said, 'Oh, poor Rodney!' That was all; but I knew by her intonation that I had been guilty of an error of taste. It was typical; so gently done, and she, who always saw the best first, left it to my good sense to understand her meaning. One day she borrowed five shillings from me. I so hoped she would forget to repay the little debt. What a joyous secret to know that Ellen Terry owed me five shillings! But after a wildly enthusiastic last performance when speeches had been made (Ellen Terry writes, 'I made a little speech which was quite a success') and she had been presented with a Life Governorship of the Shakespeare Memorial Theatre, the curtain fell and we crowded round her with our sad farewells. Suddenly she dropped my hand, and crying 'Five bob!', ran to her dressing-room and dived into that historic bag – the debt was paid!

Smallhythe was too far from London when she was acting in London. At that time she had a small Georgian house in the King's Road, Chelsea. The front door led at once into a good-sized panelled room, out of which the stairs rose to the floors above. The house had character apart from the personal charm that Ellen Terry radiated wherever she lived. One stepped out of the turmoil of the twentieth century into a period of peace that satisfied both the eye and the heart.

The first time I visited Smallhythe, I was Ellen Terry's guest for a night. When I was in bed she came to see if I had enough blankets, and then tucked me up as if I were her own son. What a wonder was that to me, being younger perhaps than my young years, to be tended by such dearness. What is it Peer Gynt cries at the end of the play? 'Mother, Wife, Holy Woman, hide me in your heart.'

I had the good fortune to work with her for two years immediately following her season at the Imperial Theatre, Westminster, where she had produced Ibsen's *The Vikings* and *Much Ado About Nothing*, under the direction of Gordon Craig. Although the season was notable and made history artistically, she lost most of her savings.

Philip Carr, who had known Ellen Terry all his life, went to see her in her dressing-room one night and, as he puts it, foolishly said something about being depressed because the theatre was not full. 'Depressed?' she cried, jumping up from the couch on which she was resting. 'My dear Phil, I have often been sad in my life and often disappointed and angry, but I have never been depressed – and I am never going to be.'

Her courage was justified, for in two years of touring she recouped her London losses. I think they were happy years for her. They certainly were for me. I had an insight into an enchanted new world, and I was admitted into a life-long friendship with one of the most magnificent women of the age.

It was a rich two years for all of us. Most of us were young, and one day, after she had finished rehearsing a difficult scene, she happened on someone reading a newspaper at the side of the stage. She gently drew down the paper so that she could see the young face, as she said, 'Can't you learn anything from our mistakes?' Once I complained of being tired at rehearsal. She whipped me with her scorn. Another time when an actor objected to the name of Jesus Christ being used in a play, she retorted, 'If you don't act for the whole glory of God, the

O

sooner you leave the stage the better.' I can imagine how she said it. It was her vowels that were so significant, and made everything she said pregnant with beauty.

Our repertory included *The Merchant of Venice, Much Ado About Nothing, The Good Hope*, and sometimes *Nance Oldfield* and scenes from *Henry VIII*.

In the church scene in *Much Ado About Nothing* she would sometimes have a little joke unobserved by the audience, which upset poor Claudio (me!), and I asked her please not to do it. 'But you play the scene so much better when you're in a temper!'

Indefatigable as she was in the theatre, she was always full of fun. Never was there anyone whose work was so part of her life, and life so part of her work, and through it all shone the steady flame of her spiritual faith.

The quality of her voice was in itself a miracle. It was soft and gentle and yet veiled with a delicious huskiness. And although it would have satisfied Lear's ideal of a woman's voice which he loved in Cordelia, its carrying power was remarkable. I recall a performance of some pageant held in the Royal Albert Hall, when many actresses of repute boomed out their little pieces in an effort to overcome the erratic acoustics and make themselves heard without success, and then on came Nance Oldfield, speaking, it would seem, quite normally, and every syllable went ringing to the uttermost back-wall of that vast arena. How often too, on a summer's evening, when sitting in Edy Craig's garden at Smallhythe, some three hundred yards from the Farm, that voice has floated on the still air, and we have known that 'Mother' has come home!

There was much of Beatrice in Ellen Terry, and not a little of the spontaneity of Rosalind: 'When I think I must speak!' At the time when she began to use a wheeled chair out of doors, there was a number of people in the garden. It was some kind of party. I was pushing the chair when a youth passed near by, and with that alert interest which never left her, she asked, 'Who's that nice-looking young man?' And then before I could answer; 'Don't tell me, I shan't remember.'

But I often think that the popular legend that she could never remember her words on the stage exaggerated. She certainly experienced difficulty in learning new words, but from my own knowledge, she never faltered in the parts she had studied when she was in her prime – for instance, in Beatrice, Portia, Queen Katharine, and Nance Oldfield. I was never conscious of any failing on my early and frequent visits to the Lyceum.

It was memorizing from the *printed* word that she found so difficult. If anyone taught her a part by sound, it was a different matter, and so when she played Hermione at His Majesty's, almost at the end of her career, her husband, James Carew, saw to it that she was word-perfect. In like manner, in the production of *The Good Hope* (Christopher St John's brilliant translation of Heijerman's play) when she played Kniertje, she and I had a difficult emotional scene lasting some twelve minutes and, although then approaching her stage Jubilee, she never forgot a word.

I am convinced that the difficulty she experienced in learning words was not because she could not memorize, but was due to her amazing vitality which could not rest. It had a quality of quicksilver. Maybe too, the written word, except in Shakespeare, was not large enough for all she wanted to express.

In wandering through the garden of my memories, I find over and over again that it is some action, some lovely movement of Ellen Terry that flashes first in my mind, and brings back the spoken word. My first vision of her in 1893, gliding on to a narrowish scene from my right – her hands pretending to cage a bird. The arresting gesture Nance Oldfield makes when declaiming Juliet's potion speech – a gesture she must have used herself when playing the part – 'Oh look! methinks I see my cousin's ghost seeking out Romeo.' Heavenly Imogen, dancing the letter scene in a delirium of happiness. 'O, for a horse with wings!' The awkward poses in the dancing lesson in *Madame Sans-Gene*, and again, the way she wiped the blood off the imaginary crown when she rated the proud sisters of Napoleon. The fire and indignation she put into that speech would have confounded those who deny that she possessed the dynamic power needed for Volumnia and Lady Macbeth. It is true that she did not employ traditional methods. In the *Daily Telegraph* criticism of her first appearance as Portia at the Prince of Wales's Theatre under the Bancrofts, the writer emphasizes her unconventional reading of the part. She had, of course, that supreme attribute of genius. She was able to discard her traditional training which she knew as well as her A B C, or use the best that was in it.

A particularly characteristic gesture of hers, which I have never seen used by anyone else, was when she would extend her two hands, one slightly in advance of the other, to indicate a direction. It was a lovely action – a flowing out through the arms to the ends of the fingers – and gave the feeling of a musical rhythm.

About the time I – aged thirteen – first fell in love with Ellen Terry I had a dream about her. I seemed to have been granted an interview, and with trembling feet I went to see her. I was ushered into a large kitchen. It was plainly furnished and whitewashed. Seated at a common deal table – that was large too – was the adored object of my visit. She was extremely busy. I cannot remember whether she was studying a part, dealing with her correspondence, or making a pudding; but she was certainly not at all pleased with me for interrupting her. Well, we are never surprised in dreams, but on reflection the whole thing seemed to me odd and very different from my expectations. But that dream strangely epitomized her character. It was like a bit out of Dunne's *Experiment in Time*. She loved simple things. She could be a perfect housewife, so why not a cook? And what was the large sitting-room at the Farm but a converted kitchen? Here was the whitewash on the plaster between the stout oak beams, the wide, ample table which might have belonged to an architect, the low, deal scholar's desk with its ink wells and hard bench attached. Schools were full of them in my day. Here she wrestled with her overwhelming correspondence which occupied so much of her spare time; and now we know from the Terry–Shaw letters what precious jewels went into the envelopes that made up the daily budget.

I remember one September evening coming back

from an expedition to see an old cottage friend of Ellen Terry's at Biddenden. He often played on a violin which he kept hanging up in a bag in the chimney. When we got there we were told that he had died. Was he able to play the violin up to the end? 'Yes,' his daughter told us, 'and de tunes he played de night he died were de best of all.'

When the wagonette got back to the Farm (yes, it was so long ago!) it was already dark. How welcome was the sight of the fire blazing on the open hearth after the drive through the cool night air. The shaded lamp lighted the table spread for a supper tempting to healthy appetites; but best of all Gandy – that's what the children named her – throws aside her wraps and with her own hands prepares in a chafing dish scrambled eggs, freshly gathered mushrooms, and other delights that we wot not of. Jupiter himself could not question the fitness of such a feast. After supper chairs are drawn to the fire; tired limbs stretched upon the cushioned settle; work-baskets, scrapbooks, pipes, and other delights are brought into the circle of the lamplight. On the dresser and high on the mantelshelf, the glistening pewter throws back the flickering flames from the logs. And then I am asked to read aloud a chapter from *Barnaby Rudge*. What an ordeal for a youngster and a new-comer to the circle!

Luckily the book is a favourite of mine and I know it pretty well, but I sweat blood, as the saying is, under the eagle eye of Edy Craig as her scissors snip a cutting for her scrapbook. For one who hopes shortly to act with Ellen Terry here is a very Atropos with her abhorred shears!

It was a stroke of genius on the part of Edy to turn the thatched barn at the Farm into a theatre as a memorial to her mother. On the anniversary of her death, when the floor is strewn with herbs and the sunlight steals in through the open door and picks out the massive beams whence a swallow maybe darts from the darkling roof-tree, it is so redolent of her gracious, joyous personality. It is a living symbol. Here, where labourers of all time, the salt of the earth, were used to toil and sweat in the eye of Phoebus, where sun-burned sickle-men, of August weary, gathered in the harvest and waited hopefully for the coming of Spring – is where we all love to re-member her and maybe tell the coming generation, our promise of spring, something of the wonder that was Ellen Terry, and how she could perform a miracle; for with her feet on the firm earth she would dance among the stars and spin gold galaxies for our delight.

Smallhythe Place, Kent

On the road to Rye, two and a half miles south of Tenterden. The Priest's House and the museum, which both date from about 1480, are half-timbered buildings with steep-pitched tiled roofs. The museum contains theatrical relics collected by Dame Ellen Terry.

GENERAL WOLFE

By Lieut-General Sir Francis Tuker

❦

ON the morning of the 13th September 1759, on the Plains of Abraham, a British general, his chest smashed by a musket-ball, staggered forward a few paces, struggling against overwhelming weakness to keep his feet. He begged a Grenadier officer close behind him to hold him up so that his men might not see him fall. 'The day is ours,' he gasped. A shattered wrist, a bullet through the groin, had not halted him. Only this last ruinous wound had brought him down.

His charging soldiers carried the battle away towards Quebec. Those about told him of his victory. 'Now God be praised, I die happy.' The tall, spare body of James Wolfe, the Soldier's Friend, Conqueror of Canada, collapsed.

It was the end he had eagerly sought, the end that he had lived for. 'A battle gained is, I believe, the highest joy mankind is capable of receiving, to him who commands.' 'The warmth of temper ... will find the way to a glorious, or at least a firm and manly end when I am of no further use to my friends and country, or when I can be serviceable by offering my life for either,' he had written to his parents, when still a young officer in his early twenties, reflective and precocious.

The death of Major-General James Wolfe was a bitter grief to his army. 'Our loss has been inconsiderable,

Quebec House, WESTERHAM, KENT

separate from our dear, courageous, yet mild Wolfe,' wrote an officer. The nation mourned as much for the loss of a great man as for the loss of a great soldier. In the north transept of Westminster Abbey is the monument dedicated to his memory by King and Parliament.

Wolfe, killed at the age of thirty-two, was the very pattern and exemplar of all that an officer should be. If any man was hatched from a cannon-ball it was James Wolfe, yet he was neither a fire-eater nor a drill sergeant, as are so many of this brood. An admirer of learning, throughout his short life he sought to acquire it and to acquaint himself with people and works of culture. He was a serious-minded, well-read student of war and of affairs. Asked to give advice to a young officer, he recommended the study of mathematics, Latin and French, and of works by Montecuculi, Feuquières, Folard, Vegetius, Thucydides, Xenophon, and a number of diverse authors with all of whom he himself was obviously well acquainted. The night before he died, as his boat dropped down the St Lawrence River, he is said to have quoted from Gray's 'Elegy' and remarked to his companions that he would rather have written that poem than win the battle that was before him.

On the 2nd January 1727, James was born at the vicarage of Westerham, Kent, where his mother was staying during her husband's absence with his regiment. The year before, the family had rented a Tudor house a little farther down the hill. It was at that house, then called Spiers, to-day known as Quebec House, that he spent the first twelve short years of his boyhood. So Quebec House is James Wolfe's home and is held in trust for the nation.

He was the elder son of Edward Wolfe, then a lieutenant-colonel, later to be promoted to lieutenant-
general, a quiet, earnest officer rather than a brilliant one.
Edward Wolfe's father and grandfather had both been
officers in the army. At the age of thirty-eight he had
married Henrietta Thompson, who came of a good
family from Marsden in Yorkshire.

There was no need to persuade James to follow his
father's calling: indeed, he was so absorbed in the idea of
soldiering from his very earliest days that he thought of
nothing else. But his parents often doubted whether his
delicate constitution would allow him to pursue the
career to which he had dedicated himself. Ill-health dogged him throughout his life. Perhaps, as with others, it
spurred him to fulfil himself quickly, while the suffering
it caused may have habituated him to face resolutely, and
to overcome, every difficulty and hardship. From that
experience may have derived his supreme moral and
physical courage, his restraint in complaining of discom-
forts, and his ability to force his frail body to endure.
Even more delicate than he, his younger brother Edward
died early of consumption while campaigning in
Belgium.

James grew to be a tall man of six feet three inches,
red-haired, thin, with a twinkle of the humour that
creates a sense of kinship between an officer and his men.

We owe most of our knowledge of Wolfe to the care
with which the Wardes, squires of Squerryes Court in
Westerham, have saved letters, commissions, and docu-
ments concerning the Wolfe family. George Warde was
James's closest friend from their very young days at Mr

Lawrence's seminary in Westerham village. He rose to be a lieutenant-general and a well-known cavalry leader of his time. He and James thought of nothing but soldiering: they played every sort of martial game that they could devise. Their infant bosoms must have been stirred to the depths by Colonel Wolfe's tales of the glorious days when he served on the Continent under the great Duke of Marlborough.

When James was twelve, the family moved to Greenwich so that Colonel Wolfe could be nearer London and to those whose patronage was necessary for his advancement, and so that his two sons could find better schooling. At Greenwich, the Revd Samuel F. Swinden undertook their education. Swinden, impressed by James's application to his work, succeeded in imparting to him his own love of learning.

By 1740 the nation, out of patience with Spanish interference with its sea-going trade, clamoured for war. An expedition was fitted out for Cartagena, and Colonel Wolfe was selected as its Adjutant-General. This was more than James's patience could bear. The thirteen-year-old schoolboy persuaded his father to let him accompany the expedition. As was expected, his health gave way almost at once while tossing at anchor in the Solent: he was returned to his school and to his lessons, thereby missing the dismal failure of the Cartagena operations.

James Wolfe suffered from seasickness far more than most men, despite his frequent experiences of sea and land operations, and his remarkable skill in exploiting them.

The great day came in November 1741, when he was

not yet fifteen. He was on holiday at Squerryes with his devoted George, when Squire Warde walked across the garden carrying an official envelope. James eagerly tore it open and, to his intense joy, found therein his first commission, from King George II, into Colonel Wolfe's regiment of Marines. Fortunately for this chronic sufferer from seasickness, the King soon afterwards commissioned him as an ensign in the 12th Foot. That very same summer he was billeted with his regiment in Flanders, fretting for a battle.

It is striking how, from this time onwards, his letters exhibit the unusual maturity of his mind, not only in his understanding of military problems but also in his comments on his own personal affairs and those of his family. Thinking and reading of war for so long had enabled him to understand his profession without being taught it. It is therefore not so strange that this stripling of sixteen was soon appointed acting adjutant of his regiment.

In June 1743, after a rigorous march, the 12th Foot found itself in Lord Stair's army near Aschaffenburg, trapped by the French between hills and river. There followed the retreat and the gallant fight and victory at Dettingen.

'Dearest Madam,' he wrote to his mother, '... our regiment has got a great deal of honour, for we were in the middle of the first line, and in the greatest danger. ...' His description of the battle to his father is as competent and matter of fact as was his cool courage during this, his first action. 'I sometimes thought that I had lost poor Ned (Edward, his brother, now serving in the same regiment) when I saw arms, legs and heads beat off close by

222

him. ... A horse I rid of the Colonel's at the first attack was shot in one of his hinder legs, and threw me: so I was obliged to do the duty of an adjutant all that and the next day on foot, in a pair of heavy boots.'

The Duke of Cumberland spoke to him several times during the day and seems never thereafter to have forgotten this lean, red-haired young enthusiast. Two weeks later the King appointed him adjutant of his regiment and promoted him to lieutenant: a year later came his captaincy in the 4th Foot. In 1745 he was a Brigade Major in the north of England, serving near his now gouty father of sixty who performed his duties seated in a coach.

The young Pretender, having taken the field, soon launched his army against General Hawley at Falkirk. James Wolfe was once more in the thick of the battle and the subsequent retreat. 'Dear Sir,' ran his letter to his Uncle Southeron, '... though we can't have been said to have totally routed the enemy, yet we remained a long time masters of the field of battle, and of our cannon, not one of which would have been lost if the drivers had not left their carriages and run off with the horses. ...'

In April of the next year this veteran of nineteen fought at Culloden. In a letter describing this battle to Major Henry Delabene he remarked, '... I have never seen an action so general, nor any victory so complete. ... The Rebels ... had orders not to give quarter to our men. We had an opportunity of avenging ourselves for that. ...' He concludes by attributing the success, not for the only time in his life, to a Higher Being.

It was here that Wolfe is said to have replied to the

Duke of Cumberland, when ordered to shoot a wounded rebel, 'My commission is at your Royal Highness's disposal, but I never can consent to become an executioner.'

By November 1746 Wolfe was off once more to join his regiment for service on the Continent. Under Cumberland, still as a Brigade Major, he fought with even greater gallantry and stubbornness at the desperately contested battle and defeat of Laffeldt. In that engagement he received a musket-ball in the body and was admitted to hospital.

During his convalescence Wolfe conceived a long-enduring passion for Miss Elizabeth Lawson, a Maid of Honour to the Princess of Wales and niece of General Mordaunt, an old friend of the Wolfe family. From the first his parents so sternly opposed the marriage that James, after much suffering, gave up the affair in compliance with their wishes, thereafter plunging all the deeper into his military studies. Not until the eve of his departure for America, the year before he died, did he transfer his affections to another woman, Miss Katherine Lowther, afterwards Duchess of Bolton. Upon her he centred all the ardour of his single-minded, single-hearted nature.

In 1749, gazetted a major, he was transferred to the 20th Foot in Scotland. Here he spent four miserable years, disliking the country, yearning for active service, in wretched health. He tried every remedy then known and suggested to him, from goat's whey to early morning cold baths, but remained a sick man. Nevertheless, the enforced inactivity had its uses. During these tedious months he was in command, devoting himself to the welfare of his officers and of his men and their families, in a manner not at that time seen in the army: training his regiment to a very high standard of discipline and of battle skill on his own successful system. For his own part he found that there was much to learn, so he became once more a student of mathematics and the classics, sitting at the feet of the professors of the University at Glasgow.

He was too observant and too conscious of his own failings to be a conceited man; at any rate those who served him did not find him so. Captain Macrae, from Glasgow in November of that year, wrote to say that, 'Our acting commander here is a paragon. He neither drinks, curses, nor runs after women. So we make him our pattern.' Wolfe's influence on the best officers in our army has been profound, if only because he was in every sense a true gentleman.

In the Highlands the good behaviour of his men, combined with his policy of bringing his officers into local society, went far to conciliate those about him who had but lately been the King's enemies. He came to admire the Highlanders' fighting spirit and advised the Government to raise battalions of these hardy men for service in America. As a result, in the summer of 1756 Pitt enlisted two Highland battalions, which later accompanied Wolfe to America.

His leisure hours he spent tramping the countryside with gun and dog or plying his salmon-rod on the river, one of the first Englishmen to exploit the sport that the Highlands had to offer. Wolfe, a lover of dogs, had always a few about him.

In 1750 he was gazetted a lieutenant-colonel of the 20th Foot. This indispensable young commander at long last obtained permission from Lord Bury, his absentee Colonel, to take leave for a visit to the Continent in order to inspect for himself the French and Prussian armies and to bring up to date his own military knowledge. He spent the months in Paris, mixing in French society only as far as was necessary to his rank and to the object of his stay. He rose early, to spend most of his day in learning to fence, ride, dance, and to talk French. Week by week his health improved with the rest and recreation.

Wolfe was an observant visitor, noting the wide gap that divided the luxury of French society from the dire poverty of the working people. He predicted trouble from the continuance of that perilous state of affairs.

After a few months, orders arrived for him to return to his regiment in Scotland; to the Highlands, to Glasgow, to the endless building of roads, to his headaches and feeble health.

In September 1753, with but six years more to live, came his release. The 20th, now esteemed 'the best in the army so far as drill and discipline go', marched south to Dover. Thence it moved to Exeter, Canterbury, Devizes, then into Gloucestershire to handle a weavers' riot. All this time its Lieutenant-Colonel was busying himself on his own improvement, reading and studying in the intervals of training. His now mature outlook is best expressed in his own words of advice to a young officer. 'I make no doubt ... you have considered yourself going into a manly profession, where you must be answerable for your own conduct; your character in life must be that of a soldier and a gentleman; the first is to be acquired by application and attendance on your duty; the second by adhering most strictly to the dictates of honour, and the rules of good breeding. ... When off duty get a sergeant or corporal, whom the adjutant will recommend to you, to teach you the exercise of the firelock, which I beg of you to make yourself as much the master of as if you were a simple soldier. ...'

A lady who knew him during his sojourn at Exeter thus described him when dancing: '... the fierceness of the soldier was absorbed in the politeness of the gentleman ... such a serene joy was diffused on his whole manners, mien, and deportment, that it gave the most agreeable turn to the features of that hero, who died for his country.' Wolfe liked the ladies. His behaviour to them was so courteous and gallant that, despite his ungainly physique, receding chin, and general lack of good looks, he certainly attracted them.

In the meanwhile the Seven Years War had broken out. Wolfe, now thirty years old, was appointed Quarter-Master-General of the expedition to Rochefort, under the command of his old friend, General Mordaunt. Dreadfully seasick during the whole operation, he showed his usual enterprise and his intolerance with inefficiency and inactivity. He had himself rowed ashore and, after reconnaissance, strenuously urged a plan of attack to complete the first phase of the taking of Rochefort. Naval and military commanders agreed, then, having launched the soldiers to the assault, took fright and recalled them while still in the boats. The expedition was abortive, solely because of the hesitation and lack of courage of its senior officers.

'We shall return to England with reproach and dishonour,' wrote Wolfe, 'though in my mind, there never was in any troops, sea and land, a better disposition to serve.'

Inglorious, the fleet and soldiers sailed home to England. Arrived there, Wolfe had the unenviable role of giving evidence at the Board of Inquiry that examined Mordaunt's conduct: the outcome was a court-martial and acquittal for Mordaunt, but a commendation for Wolfe whose name was now prominent before King and people.

The news from America was even more gloomy, for Montcalm, after taking Fort William Henry, had allowed his Red Indians to massacre the garrison treacherously in cold blood. These things shocked Wolfe and left him thirsting for revenge on the French. Chatham, planning a counter-offensive, sent for Amherst to lead an expedition and for Whitmore, Laurence, and Wolfe to command its brigades. Summoned to London from the west country, Wolfe covered 170 miles over poor roads in thirty-one hours, to be rewarded on his arrival with the commission of a brigadier.

In February he and his men were aboard, only to toss for a week in the Channel with contrary winds, so that it was not until the 2nd June that Louisbourg, their first and chief objective, hove in sight. No time was lost. At night on the 7th June Wolfe's brigade of Grenadiers, Highlanders, and Light Infantry embarked in their boats to launch the main assault. At dawn in a choppy sea with a heavy surf, the boats were met full in the face by a blast of artillery fire. Wolfe's flagstaff was shot away. One boatload of Light Infantrymen found a landing-place and Wolfe, standing erect in his boat, waved the rest on to follow them. Cane in hand he jumped into the surf, made land, and set about organizing his force as the men leapt ashore cheering him as they came. A few feet above his head a battery blew gaps in the ranks. In the teeth of it, the indomitable Brigadier succeeded in forming up a sufficient force for attack. At the head of his troops, he led the assault on the first battery, carried it, and pressed on to the French entrenchments. By now, seeing Laurence's brigade moving up in support of the intrepid Wolfe, their retreat threatened, the enemy fled.

Wolfe followed and took position before the walls of Louisbourg. From now onwards his was the leading, aggressive spirit that pressed forward the engineering works, the batteries, and the assaulting troops until, on the 25th July, Admiral Boscawen's boarding-party seized the last of the French defending vessels in the harbour. Drocour thereupon surrendered Louisbourg, a fortress till then deemed to be impregnable.

Wolfe at once urged for an attack on Quebec before winter set in. Those above him refused to move, so, in serious ill-health, he sailed that autumn for leave in England. As he travelled home Pitt's despatch, ordering the offensive against Quebec for 1759 and placing James Wolfe in command, passed him on the high seas.

No sooner had he set foot in England than he made straight for Salisbury to be with the 67th Foot of which he was now the Colonel. But his fame had flown before him.

He was soon called to London for an interview with the Secretary of State. There Wolfe received his commission as a Major-General, together with orders to return to America to command the operations against Quebec. His naval colleague was to be Admiral Saunders, a bold, enterprising sailor, a man after Wolfe's own heart.

The story goes that Pitt gave a dinner in London, during which a distinguished guest was amazed at Wolfe's unusually theatrical behaviour. Newcastle, getting wind of this, ran to George the Third declaring that Wolfe was mad and unfit for high command. The King's retort, 'Mad, is he? Then I hope he will bite some of my other generals,' is almost as well known as the soldier concerning whom it was made.

On the 13th May 1759 Wolfe and Saunders were off Louisbourg. There Wolfe learnt of his father's death, a calamity that was not unexpected. Habituated to the idea of death, he set grief aside and plunged into his work. In a letter to his uncle, Major Walter Wolfe, the young general compiled a masterly analysis of the situation as it would be when he reached Quebec, anticipating that with forces about equal to his enemy he must be prepared for heavy fighting downstream to obtain a crossing over the Charles River, and forecasting the probability of a landing above the city and an attack from that direction. So matters turned out.

On the 26th June, the fleet having anchored four miles down river from Quebec, Wolfe went ashore to examine the enemy's dispositions. His first project was to land downstream and force the passages of the Rivers Montmorenci and Charles, thus compelling the French to abandon their strong fortifications outside the city and meet him in open battle. Prosecuting this plan, the British forces landed. On the 31st July, preparations completed, they attacked to force the crossing of the Montmorenci, only to be thrown back after a bloody fight. Five weeks of toil seemed to have been wasted. Wolfe now decided to pass his main force secretly up river and to land above Quebec, thereby threatening the town on its most weakly defended side. By the movements of Saunders' ships, by artillery bombardment, and other feints he kept his enemy's attention diverted towards an attack below Quebec. He thus planned to hustle Montcalm into an open battle, unsupported by his scattered detachments.

James Wolfe, now desperately ill, rallied his strength for the task ahead. By night, the fleet sailed past Quebec. He was rowed ashore to reconnoitre. On careful inspection, with unerring tactical insight, he selected the point of landing at the foot of a steep cliff up which he decided it was possible for his men to clamber undetected. They would then fall upon the weak and unsuspecting French pickets above.

In the darkness of the early morning of the 13th September 1759 his regiments floated silently down the St Lawrence. Wolfe launched his Highlanders up the precipitous ascent. At dawn he formed his force for battle on the plain above, in itself a brilliant operation in the circumstances. As he had designed it, his daring approach drew Montcalm into the open field to face unaided the defeat that the British Commander had doggedly prepared for him.

Before and after Wolfe, great commanders have beaten their enemy by planning to do what seemed impossible to any but the most highly skilled military artist. They have relied on their opponents' conviction that the course selected would indeed be impossible. Wolfe did more than this, for even his own brigadiers openly expressed their lack of faith in his plans. This is the absolute measure of Wolfe's moral courage and greatness as a commander. With his reputation and his whole career as the stake, he backed his judgement, and he won.

Quebec House, Kent

At the junction of the Edenbridge and Sevenoaks roads in Westerham. A square, brick house, probably early sixteenth century in origin, now mainly of the seventeenth century. The principal rooms, with a collection of 'Wolfiana', are shown at certain times.

Q

Wordsworth's House, COCKERMOUTH, CUMBERLAND

WILLIAM · WORDSWORTH

By Norman Nicholson

WILLIAM WORDSWORTH was a true northerner. On both his father's side and his mother's he was largely of Scandinavian stock, and he showed the physical and psychological characteristics of a strain which, as late as the eighteenth century, was still markedly different from that of the rest of England. Those characteristics were a tall, lean body, and a mind capable of strong passions, yet always tending to hide them beneath reserve. His father's family came from Penistone in Yorkshire, while his mother, Anne Cookson, was the daughter of a mercer at Penrith. The Cooksons, like the Wordsworths, were of Yorkshire descent, though the grandmother was one of the Crackanthorpes of Newbiggin Hall, who derived, no doubt, from the Vikings who had colonized the dales in the eighth and ninth centuries. They were one of the oldest families in the district, and their descendants still live at Newbiggin Hall, where there is an amusing rhyme carved on a wall which suggests that one of Wordsworth's ancestors faintly anticipated his genius: –

> Christopher Crackanthorpe men did me call,
> Who in my time did build this hall,
> And framed it as you may see
> In one thousand, one hundred, thirty and three.

William Wordsworth was born at Cockermouth on

the 7th April 1770. The town, taking its name from the River Cocker, which here flows into the Derwent, lies in the narrow band of mountain limestone that divides the Lake District proper from the farming country of the Carlisle Plain. Northward it looks to the old Forest of Inglewood and all the history and ballads of the Border; and southward it looks to the fells. The castle was a defence against the Scots in the time when the county was never really free from wars and raids; while the fells stood as a much more effective defence of valleys which at the end of the eighteenth century had scarcely been disturbed by a stranger for nearly 1000 years.

Cockermouth is linked, also, to the mining district of West Cumberland, for nearer the coast this mountain limestone bears large deposits of iron ore, with, close beside them, the coalfields of Whitehaven and Workington. So the town is at the junction of the three types of country and of the three ways of life which play an essential part in the history of the Cumberland people: Inglewood and the farmers, the coast and the miners, and the fells and the dalesmen. In Worthsworth's day it must have been a busy little town of streets, warehouses, and inns, with a few thousand inhabitants crowded into narrow alleys and courts opening off the High Street. John Wordsworth, in his capacity of law-agent to Sir John Lowther, lived in a large Georgian house set back a dozen yards or so from the main street. It is solid and imposing rather than elegant, and at the back there is an almost-square walled garden, leading to a paved terrace which runs beside the river. Here, one feels, was where the children of the landlord's agent would play, rather than in the street with the ragged village boys. Here, too, Wordsworth felt his first animal response to nature. The Derwent, he says: –

> ' ... loved
> To blend his murmurs with my nurse's song,
> And, from his alder shades and rocky falls,
> And from his fords and shallows, sent a voice
> That flowed along my dreams.'
> (*Prelude*, Book 1)

A little later in the same passage he describes his childhood at Cockermouth, painting a scene which in its variety, its bright colours, its hint of near-urban chatter and cheerfulness, is almost unique in his work: –

> 'Oh, many a time have I, a five years' child,
> In a small mill-race severed from his stream,
> Made one long bathing of a summer's day;
> Basked in the sun, and plunged and basked again
> Alternate, all a summer's day, or scoured
> The sandy fields, leaping through flowery groves
> Of yellow ragwort; or when rock and hill,
> The woods, and distant Skiddaw's lofty height,
> Were bronzed with deepest radiance, stood alone
> Beneath the sky, as if I had been born
> On Indian plains, and from my mother's hut
> Had run abroad in wantonness, to sport,
> A naked savage, in the thunder shower.'

The mention of Skiddaw reminds us that the first fells that Wordsworth knew were not the rather fussy hills around Windermere, nor even the great crags of Coniston and Langdale, but those huge, solid lumps of rock around Bassenthwaite and Buttermere: Skiddaw, Saddleback, Grasmoor, Melbrake. They are all fells of the rock known as Skiddaw Slate, and they are bare, plain, and animal-like, very different from the soaring pikes and pinnacles of the central dales. I believe that these great mountain forms so impressed themselves on the boy's mind that they provided the basic imagery for his poetry. They overshadow much of his finest work as the 'huge peak, black and huge' overshadowed the boy in the boat on Ullswater. Often when his mind was stirred to deepest thought, he saw before him the 'huge stone', the 'sounding cataract', dreary moors, and 'dark and gloomy woods'.

When Wordsworth was eight his mother died and he went to live with his grandparents at Penrith. Here he was unhappy, probably grieving for Cockermouth and the Derwent, and resenting the somewhat repressive discipline of his grandfather. He became unsociable, violent in temper, and even contemplated suicide. Luckily he had not to spend much time there, for he now entered Hawkshead Grammar School, boarding out at Anne Tyson's cottage in the village. Hawkshead, once a centre of the Lancashire and Westmorland wool trade, is a small town in the shallow valley that lies between Windermere and Coniston. Here, outside school hours, he was as free as a gipsy. He would encircle Esthwaite Lake in the morning, and, in the afternoon, would go bathing in summer or skating in winter. And on half-day holidays he would take a boat on Windermere, or ride to Furness Abbey and the Ulverston Sands, or walk over Walna Scar to fish in the Duddon. It was a time of intense happiness. The boy then felt a communion with nature which was all the greater because the experience was untroubled by 'the meddling intellect'. He heard, it is true, no murmur of 'the still, sad music of humanity'; he felt no hint of a mystical understanding, no

'... sense sublime
Of something far more deeply interfused.'

But he accepted nature completely and unreservedly, accepted the sky and the air and the rain as unquestioningly as a flower or a bird accepts them. His senses breathed life in at every pore; they stored up experience as a daffodil stores up sunlight, and for the rest of his life his spirit drew strength from this hidden food.

But schooldays could not last for ever, and in 1787 Wordsworth entered St John's College, Cambridge. Here he found it very difficult to adjust himself to the change, for now he was in a new and strange society, mostly of rich and rather idle young men, among whom he felt gawky and inexperienced – a provincial with no money, no polish, and a broad northern accent. Nor was his self-confidence strengthened by his indecision about the future. His father had died in 1783, leaving the four children (Richard, William, Dorothy, and John) with little more than a claim on the Lowther estate for about £5000, which the debtor refused to pay. Probably Wordsworth resented this, and felt that society was withholding from him the start in life which was his proper due. This, together with his earlier enjoyment of the free life of Hawkshead, made him impatient of authority and ready to listen sympathetically to the idea of revolution.

He visited the Continent on a walking tour in the summer of 1790, and when he left Cambridge the following year he turned again to France. There, in Orleans, he met Michael Beaupuis and Annette Vallon, both of whom influenced him very deeply. From Beaupuis he learned the democratic principles of which he had already caught a glimpse in the lives of the 'statesmen' of Cumberland ('a perfect republic of shepherds and agriculturalists', he said in his *Guide to the Lakes*). And from Annette he learned the full force of passionate love. She was twenty-six at this time and he was twenty-two. We know little about the beginning of their love for one another, but soon Annette was expecting a child. In the spring of 1792 she went to Blois to stay with her mother and stepfather, but in September she returned to Orleans for her confinement. Wordsworth remained with her until the end of October when he went to Paris, from whence, having waited until he had heard of the birth of his child (on the 15th December), he rushed across to England.

In their anxiety to hush up this affair, Wordsworth's family and his official biographers seem to have hidden much that might have helped us to understand his conduct at this time. Perhaps it is not so discreditable as it seems. Probably, indeed, he hoped to persuade his family to accept Annette, and perhaps to provide for her and the child until he could make a career for himself. But if this was his plan he got no chance to carry it out, for in February 1793 France declared war on England, and the personal difficulties of the two lovers were swallowed up in the national calamity.

The next few years were the blackest in Wordsworth's life. The war separated him from Annette, though there is evidence to suggest that he may have made a desperate attempt to see her in the autumn of 1793, getting across

to France, and even as far as Paris, before the outbreak
of the Reign of Terror forced him to return. But he soon
began to realize that though Annette had swept him off
his feet for a few months, there was little but physical
passion between them. And as the war dragged on year
after year, the passion left him, and (in spite of strong
feelings of guilt and obligation to Annette and to their
child) his thoughts began to turn once again to Mary
Hutchinson, whom he had known as a boy at Penrith.
Moreover, as his love for Annette waned so did his sympathy for France. His first revolutionary fervour had been
checked when Robespierre came into power, and now
he had to acknowledge that the cause of Liberty, Equality, and Fraternity had turned into a new despotism. All
his hopes, political as well as personal, his faith in man
and his faith in himself, seemed to give way under him,
and he descended into a deep pit of disillusion, despair,
remorse, and purposelessness.

From all this it was Dorothy, more than any other human being, who helped to rescue him. She filled the gap
which had been left by Annette; she gave him sympathy,
trust, and, above all, belief in himself. There is no doubt
that her love for him was the most important emotional
force in her life, and because it could never be fulfilled in
the normal physical way, it was bound to be in part frus-
trated, and may have been the cause of her final break-
down. In those first years together there was an im-
mensely subtle and delicate understanding between
them. They were, to adapt a phrase of Coleridge's, 'two
persons and one soul'. For a while they stayed at Windy
Brow, a farmhouse near Keswick, living a hand-to-

mouth existence on next to nothing. Then Raisley Cal-
vert, whom Wordsworth had nursed in an illness, died
and left him £900, with which in September 1795 they
were able to settle on their own at Racedown in Dorset.
Here they came into contact with Coleridge, and the
match was set to a fire that has not yet gone out.

It is probable that Coleridge was important to Wordsworth more as an encouragement than as an example.
The ideas and even the style of the mature Wordsworth
had already begun to show in the poems written before
his friendship with Coleridge. During the years of despair his mind had gone back to his childhood at Cockermouth and Hawkshead, and in these memories he found
a new joy and peace. At the same time, his feeling for his
fellow men (for the failure of the French Revolution
had not robbed him of this) made him turn to the language and lives of simple, ordinary people for the material of his poetry. It was from such material – ordinary
people, ordinary speech, and the world of nature – that
Lyrical Ballads were formed.

Their effect was revolutionary, and is still felt to-day.
Wordsworth had realized that the conventional poetic
diction of the eighteenth century was grown over with
second-hand associations, second-hand meanings, and
that he must scrape it clean again. He wanted to pick up
the ordinary, everyday words which he found lying
about him like pebbles – to pick them up and pile them
together and let the wind blow through them. It was a
job which simply had to be done before his new sort of
poetry could be written, and, indeed, before any new
poetry could be written. If no one had made the

experiments in language which Wordsworth made, scarcely any of the new poetry of the nineteenth and twentieth centuries could have been written.

In December 1799 Wordsworth and his sister went to live at Dove Cottage in Grasmere, formerly a public-house. Much of the finest of his work was produced there – *Michael*, *Resolution and Independence*, the immortality *Ode*, and most of the *Prelude*. Yet it is a mistake to regard the Grasmere district as one of the formative influences behind his work. He was already a mature poet before he went there: he had found his style and he knew what he wanted to say. Grasmere added little to the vital experience out of which his poetry came, but it did give him the opportunity to put that poetry into words. Grasmere was his workshop. There at Dove Cottage, living very cheaply, and in almost complete isolation, he poured out poem after poem. He and his sister ate and slept in the cottage, but otherwise lived out of doors, wandering about Easedale and Langdale, or walking by Dunmail Raise and Watendlath to Derwentwater and Keswick. Even the poetry was composed (or, as it sometimes seemed, *gathered*) outside, and put on paper afterwards in the evenings at the cottage.

But after a few years the vision which had sustained him, like the sacrament sustains a fasting saint, began to fade and decline, and the poet looked down the dale to the comfortable landscape of Rydal and Windermere. Mr Herbert Read has argued that the main reason for this decline was remorse for his desertion of Annette, but there are other factors which have to be considered. To begin with, Wordsworth was already ageing – at thirty-nine he looked sixty – and his sensual response to nature was getting fainter and less compulsive. In 1802 (having first visited France with Dorothy to close the books with Annette) he married Mary Hutchinson, and, though the marriage brought him comfort and happiness, it was not the sort to exalt or even to provoke a man into poetry. Moreover, it meant inevitably a break between Wordsworth and his sister: there was no estrangement, but the perfect consonance of Racedown and the first years at Dove Cottage was never quite repeated. Nor was this the only loss: first he quarrelled with Coleridge, and then, in 1805, John Wordsworth, the younger brother, was drowned off the coast of Weymouth, and his death was deeply felt by both William and Dorothy. Again, marriage had brought responsibilities. By this time, following the death of the first Lord Lonsdale, the Wordsworths had received their share of the estate, but a growing family needed a larger house and a larger income. He found the first, after several intermittent flittings, in Rydal Mount, and the latter in the sinecure office of Distributor of Stamps for Westmorland. Gradually he settled down into a comfortable, sedate middle age.

There is no need to begrudge him any of this – he had given himself to his vision while it lasted, and now he had a right to rest and retirement. But this accession to respectability was marked by a change of views which angered his younger contemporaries, making them speak contemptuously of Wordsworth's 'apostacy'. Certainly it is ironic that the former revolutionary and deist should now have become a die-hard Tory, a Little Englander, and a bigotted supporter of the Established

Church. Deprived of his poetic vision, Wordsworth's love of his native district narrowed into parochialism and his feeling for the continuity of natural phenomena hardened into a short-sighted conservatism.

He outlived all his contemporaries and survived the first enthusiasm of his disciples, and he began to feel isolated, left behind in a new age of literature which he himself had done more than anyone to form. Dorothy now was lost to him in a pathetic senility, and Dora, his favourite child, died in 1847. He was very famous, of course, widely read, and greatly honoured (in 1843 he had been made Poet Laureate), but we feel that this did not compensate for the loss of Coleridge's splendid trust and the fierce fighting spirit of 1797. During his last ten or twenty years he led a strange, almost posthumous, life, lit only by an after-glow of poetry, so that many of his more perceptive admirers must have thought sometimes that it might have been better for his reputation if he had died at forty. But they need not have worried: his greatest poem, the *Prelude*, was yet to be published, and with the death of the old Wordsworth in 1850, the young Wordsworth came alive for ever.

Wordsworth House, Cumberland

On the north side of the main street of the village of Cockermouth. A many-windowed house with the original staircase, fire places, and panelling of 1745. It is now used as an antiquarian book-shop.